Jacob K. Jones

A Brief History of the Methodist Episcopal Church of Spring City, Pa.

together with, Sketches of the other leading churches of the town

Jacob K. Jones

A Brief History of the Methodist Episcopal Church of Spring City, Pa.
together with, Sketches of the other leading churches of the town

ISBN/EAN: 9783337369545

Printed in Europe, USA, Canada, Australia, Japan

Cover: Foto ©Lupo / pixelio.de

More available books at **www.hansebooks.com**

1845   1899

A BRIEF HISTORY

of the

Methodist Episcopal Church

Of Spring City, Pa.,

Together with

SKETCHES OF THE OTHER LEADING CHURCHES OF THE TOWN

—

COMPILED BY J. K. JONES, M. E.

June, 1899.

PREFACE.

At a Quarterly Conference of the Methodist Episcopal Church held at Spring City, Pa., January 23, 1897, the author of this little volume was appointed to write up the history of the Spring City Methodist Episcopal Church. Had it not been for the admiration he has for the church of his choice, and for the ardent love which he has for the Lord, he could not have been induced to undertake such a laborious task. In many cases the records of the church are not to be found. This then gave rise to an additional source of anxiety, since the memory of those of longest existence hereabouts had to be so frequently consulted. In many instances people differ greatly in their remembrance of the dates and facts connected with certain events. An earnest effort has been made to sift the truth from these sources, and to tell it in language which is devoid of high-sounding technicalities.

The aim has been to present to the readers of this volume, in as compact form as possible, a collection of material for future reference, as well as for present perusal. Many of the facts herein contained would, in a few years, forever have been buried in oblivion. Accuracy of facts and dates has also been attempted. In some cases the aim of the author here may not have been fully carried out; but, in the main, we think that the material as here presented may be accepted as correct.

We trust that our readers will not think the sketches of the other churches are out of place. We all read the same Bible, trust in the same Saviour, and are striving to gain an entrance to the same Heaven. An outline of the beginnings of things is also given. These may be of interest to some people.

Our acknowledgments are due to Messrs. John Finkbiner, W. C. Taylor, Davis Hause, Esq., of West Chester, the ministers of the churches, and to all others who have so willingly lent their services in gathering the materials from which our story has been woven.

May we trust that you will receive the book in the same kind, generous spirit in which it has been written? That the spiritual life of its readers may be quickened, and the cause of the Master promoted, is the earnest wish of the author.

J. K. J.

JACOB K. JONES, M. E.
INSERTED BY SPECIAL REQUEST OF COMMITTEE

CHAPTER I.

THE BEGINNINGS.

TITLE.

Originally the land in this vicinity was a part of the Old William Penn Grant. As early as 1682 we find that Professor Thomas Holme, surveyor general of William Penn, made a map of the "Improved Parts of Pennsylvania." In this map the sections now included in the Vincent Townships are given in the names of "Sr. Matthias Vincent, Adrian Vrouzen, Benja, Furloy, Dr. Daniel Coxe." On November 22, 1686, Dr. Daniel Coxe of London "being siezed of a tract of 10,-000 acres in Pennsylvania, lying between two rivers, called Vincent River, and Schuylkill River, ordered the same to be divided into two equal parts, each containing 5000 acres." From the 5000 acres along the "Schuylkill" River he granted 1000 acres to a Mr. John Clapp, "of the Province of Carolina, in America." For this land Mr. Clapp was to pay to the said Daniel Coxe "a grain of corn yearly for the first six years, and afterward the yearly rent of £4 6s."

The Vincent River referred to above is now French Creek. This region hereabouts took its name from "Sr. Matthias Vincent." The land was known for a number of years as "Coxe and Company's 20,000 acres." The earliest settlers of the Vincents were soon supplanted by the Germans, many of whose descendants still are in possession of the lands which have been handed down through the lapse of years. Among the names of these early land owners we find

those of Ralston, Gordon, Dennis, Whelen, and Bromback
(now corrupted by Brownback).

In 1738 by order of the court of Chester County a survey
of the Vincents was made, and the following boundaries are
recorded—"Northeast by Schuylkill River, Northwest by
Nantmeal and Coventry, Southwest by Uwchlan, and South-
east by Joseph Pike's land," now Pikeland.

A NATURAL CAVE.

In 1773, just three years before the Revolutionary War
broke out, another survey and draft of the township was
made. On this draft reference is made to a Natural Cave.
It is described and located as being near the Schuylkill River,
and just opposite the lower end of the island; but within the
boundaries of what is now Spring City. This cave was known
as "Bezalion's Cave," and it must have been somewhere in
the hill about the Paper Mill. As there is no trace of the
cave now visible, it was no doubt obliterated in excavating
for the canal or the Paper Mill.

This cavern was named after a French Indian fur trader
by the name of Pierre (Peter) Bezalion, who at times located
hereabouts, and bartered with the Indians for furs of various
kinds, during the early days of the eighteenth century. It
is supposed that Mr. Bezalion discovered the cave. He, at
least, knew about it, and perhaps at times, lodged therein,
and kept some of the furs there also.

This French trader is represented as one of the most
noted of his craft in the whole province. He, at times, pene-
trated far into the interior of the State in quest of pelts.
About the year 1724, after collecting considerable pelf, he
left this region, and settled on a tract of land east of Coates-

ville. There he remained until his death in 1742, at which time he was able to leave to his heirs a tract of 158 acres of land, valued at about Twenty-five Hundred Dollars.

The Indians of that day in this region were numerous, the streams swarmed with fish, and the forests abounded with game and wild animals. These Red Skins belonged to the tribe of Lenni Lenape, or Delawares. They did a good business in trapping and hunting, but the white fur traders secured the greatest income from the business. These Indians called French Creek Sankanac, the Perkiomen Pahkiomink, and the Schuylkill Manaiunk.

First Houses.

By the year 1837 the Schuylkill Canal was in operation, and had been since about 1825. The Reading Railroad was fast nearing completion. It began carrying passengers and traffic about 1839. As some of my older readers may remember, the road, under the name of the "Philadelphia, Germantown, and Norristown Railroad," was finished in 1832. In the beginning of this year, 1837, but two houses were here, one, at the Locks below where Mr. A. F. Tyson's store now stands, and the other near by.

But, during this summer the first houses, three in number, all of stone, all nearly alike constructed, were built on what is now North Main Street. These houses are still under roof. One of them, No. 123, stands near the canal, and it was built by Mr. Samuel Quig. Another, now a part of Mr. P. H. Setzler's restaurant, No. 120, was built by Mr. Peter Quig. The third, No. 104, owned by Dr. W. Brower, was built by John Speace.

NAME.

Back in the fifties people began to cast about for a name for the little village as it began to be. An effort was made by some to have the place called Jamestown, but the attempt did not succeed. Many of our readers well remember the beautiful spring, under a large willow-tree, which was on Main Street at the foot of Yost Avenue. A pump still brings the water of this spring up to slake the thirst of the thirsty. On account of this, and other springs about this region, the name of Springville was selected. This name was retained until the year 1872, when an effort prevailed to have the name changed to Spring City. This change was made to correspond with the post-office which was then called by that name. The first borough census, taken in 1870, showed that 1112 souls were in the borough.

STORES.

About the year 1835 James Rogers, Sr., built a small, frame, store-house near the Locks. This was at Royer's Locks, and the greater part of the custom came from supplying the boatmen. This store was kept open for business *seven days in the week*, and corn, oats, groceries, rum, gin, brandy, and whisky were sold to *everybody*, young and old alike.

Some time afterward a second store was built by Mr. David Royer, about where the Pennsylvania Railroad siding now crosses the canal.

RIVER BRIDGE.

The Royer's Ford Bridge Company was chartered May 1, 1839. During that year and 1840 the first bridge, a wooden,

RIVER BRIDGE, EAST VIEW

covered structure, was thrown across the river, at a cost of $8500. This structure which was a toll bridge, safely carried its passengers and traffic until the large freshet of September 2, 1850, lifted it from the piers, and carried it down to Black Rock Tunnel. The bridge was immediately replaced by a structure of similar pattern. This second bridge, which cost $8000, did service until the night of May 4, 1884, a fire which originated in the Yost grist mill, at its west end, swept the bridge and the mill away.

The present iron structure was then erected at a cost of $13,000. The contract of erection was done by the Phœnix Bridge Company of Phœnixville. In the year 1887 the County Commissioners of both Chester and Montgomery counties, purchased the interests of the stockholders for $33,-500, and declared the bridge free of toll.

STOVE FOUNDRIES.

The first stove foundry of the place was built by James Rogers, Sr., about the year 1843. This plant stood on the canal bank along below Mr. John Macfeat's stove store, and from this place south toward the Lyceum. It was surrounded by the first lumberyard of the place. A high board fence along the east side of Main Street shut off the view from the street.

The foundry employed about 25 hands, and made the old-fashioned nine-plate wood stoves. Afterward cook stoves and hydraulic rams for raising water, were also made here. The supplies were at first brought on the canal, then on the railroad.

On the evening of April 30, 1856, a fire in the engine-room was discovered by a passing boatman who gave the alarm. By the time the people were aroused the fire was beyond control, and this wooden structure went up in smoke, and it was never rebuilt.

Four years now elapsed before another attempt at stove making was made. But in 1860 the people contributed means, and a second foundry was erected on the site now occupied by the Yeager-Hunter Stove Works. This plant was operated during the Rebellion by the firm of Smith, Francis & Wells; then by Smith, Johnson & Co.; and afterward by the firm of Shantz & Keeley. On July 5, 1881, a fire again checked the stove industry of Spring City, as the entire plant, then a large one, was swept from existence.

Then in 1883 the present plant was erected on the ruins of the old site, by contributions as before. The business firm of Yeager & Hunter then leased and operated the works for ten years, when the above firm purchased the grounds and the entire plant. In 1890 the business was incorporated under the firm title of the "Yeager-Hunter Spring City Stove Works." The business now employs about one hundred hands.

THE PAPER MILL.

The title to the paper mill property was conveyed by Mr. Frederick Yost to Messrs. Shryock & Co., April 9, 1847. The mill, a small one, was then erected, and operated by several firms in succession. Here are some of the firm names—Messrs. Shryock, Paxson & Knight; Messrs. Nixson & Co.; Messrs. Bursler & Stearley; Mr. William Shearer; Messrs. Burgess, Keen & Ladd; and, from about the year 1864, The American Wood Paper Company, a stock company, managed the business. Mr. Hugh Burgess was President of the Company.

At first wrapping paper only was made, and this, generally from straw. But, after a series of experiments, paper and paper pulp were made at this mill from poplar wood. Then the business, which up to this time had not been so productive in financial results, greatly flourished. The first consignment of wood paper pulp, one ton, was shipped in 1862 to Mr. James McGargee, then a paper maker on the Wissahickon Creek, several miles above Philadelphia.

About 25 hands were employed at the mill at first; but, when the works shut down indefinitely in 1893, the names of 125 persons were on the pay roll. This mill, in its bright days, did a great deal for the material growth of the town.

PUBLIC HALLS.

I. THE LYCEUM.

"Springville Lyceum, 1842," were the words that ornamented a painted board which had been placed over the door of a building, now a dwelling, Nos. 3 and 5 North Main Street, and owned by Mr. Jesse G. Yeager. This historic building was erected by Mr. James Rogers, Sr., in the year above named. The lower story was a dwelling, and the upper story was used for public purposes. The public room was about 32 by 35 feet in size. The entrance was by a door from Main Street, which opened into a small vestibule. From this vestibule a flight of stairs led to the upper room. Imagine yourself entering from the street, then turn to the left a few steps, now turn to the right, and ascend the steps as though you are going toward the canal. You have the idea.

The stairway at the top was protected by a baluster. The room extended East and West, and the speaking stand was at the East end, or end next the canal. A sort of box-like arrangement about 8 or 10 feet long and 4 feet high extended partly across the room, and this served as the speaker's desk. Two windows, one near each end of the speaker's stand, but back of it, admitted the light at that end of the room. At first there were no regular seating accommodations. Nail kegs were placed about the room on which boards were laid. On these improvised seats the people at first sat. But, as time wore on a few benches were placed. Along the sides of the room a few benches extended lengthwise, so that when those who occupied them wished to see the speaker, they were obliged to turn partly around; that is, the audience along the North and the South side of the room sat sideways, or at right angles to the speaker. In the centre of the room, a few benches extended cross-wise. The speaker's stand was painted yellow.

Now as to the means of lighting the room for evenings. My older readers will have no trouble to understand this; but the younger folks must now draw on their imagination, while we shall attempt to describe. Can you imagine a piece of inch board ten or twelve inches long, and four or five inches wide, with another piece of the same width, and four inches long nailed against the bottom of the long piece, and at right angles to it? If so, now imagine an auger hole bored half way through the botton piece and you have the candlestick used in the "Lyceum." A half-inch hole in the top of our candlestick will serve to suspend it. A dozen or fifteen of these "home-made" devices, each with a piece of a "tallow-dip," made in some nearby home, in it, were all the means of giving light to this historic room for evening services. Now see some person with a pair of snuffers in one hand passing around every few minutes during a meeting. With the other hand he lifts our candlestick off its nail support, clips

off the charred wick, dresses up the wick a little, and replaces
the newly brightened light again on its nail. Or, if the
snuffers are not in easy reach, some one near by takes the
candle out of its socket, and with his pocket knife he cuts
off the wick against the end of a post or a bench. Or per-
chance he, with a moistened thumb and forefinger, pinches
the burned wick off. Near the close of the Lyceum's existence a couple of whale oil lamps were placed back of the
pulpit against the wall. This was an improvement.

We have dwelt at some length on this historic spot on
account of its significance. In the ten years of its life as a
public hall it was the only place of its kind in the growing
village. In that upper room were held the first Sunday-
Schools, the first day schools both public and private, also the
first preaching services. Aside from these services, debating
societies, lectures, and town meetings generally were held
here until about the year 1852, when a more ample provision
was made for the public gatherings of the town.

II. MECHANICS' HALL.

By the end of ten years from the time the Lyceum had
been built, the needs of a larger and a better adapted building were apparent in which to hold the public concourses.
The Order of United American Mechanics took up the work
in the year 1852, and erected of stone, on Hall Street, the
building which still does public service. This was the second
public hall. It served its mission until the year 1878 when
it was remodeled and made to suit more comfortably the increasing demands of the public.

The greater part of the public assemblies then met in
this hall, and finally the Lyceum was converted into a dwelling, and Mechanics' Hall naturally became the place for hold-

ing the public demonstrations of the town. Besides the gatherings which congregate in the hall proper to-day, 1899, quite a number of beneficial orders meet in lodge rooms on the third floor. We hereby present a list of these assemblies as they are now assembling:—

Monday evening.—I. O. of Red Men, Pickering Tribe, No. 13. Jr. O. U. A. M., No. 900.

Tuesday evening.—P. O. S. of A., No. 122. Phœnix Encampment of Patriarchs, No. 79.

Wednesday evening.—P. O. S. of A., No. 191.

Thursday evening.—I. O. of O. F., No. 762. D. of L., No. 101.

Friday evening.—K. of P., No. 91. The Iron-molders' Union, No. 75.

Saturday evening.—O. U. A. M., No. 76.

III. MEMORIAL HALL.

The third public hall, known as Memorial Hall, was finished and dedicated on May 10, 1894. This pretty and convenient structure is also of stone, and it stands on Chestnut Street. Some of the papers read at the dedication were: "Presentation of the Keys," by Rev. F. C. Yost; "Acceptance of the Keys," by Rev. Calvin U. O. Derr, Pastor of the First Reformed Church, Spring City; "Links Between the Church and the Young People," by Rev. C. H. Coons; "The Moral and Spiritual Results of the Institutional Church," by Dr. James I. Good, and "What the World Expects of the Church," by F. G. Hobson, Esq.

Memorial Hall is the munificent gift of the late Mr. Henry Francis, a liberal, public-spirited gentleman of the First Reformed Church of Spring City. The hall is 40 feet

MEMORIAL HALL

by 70 feet, three stories high, and it cost about $10,000 all told. A well-equipped gymnasium occupies the third-story, and a fine lecture room with a seating capacity of 300 is on the second-story. On the first floor are a Ladies' parlor, Boys' game room, Reading room, Kitchen and banquet room. The following persons contributed liberally in furnishing the auxiliary rooms: Mrs. Mary E. Keeley, Mrs. W. P. Snyder, and Mrs. Clara (Keeley) Derr.

A well-conducted, and well-attended popular lecture course was started in the fall of 1884, and it has been kept up regularly since. This course of entertainments is doing much for the literary and æsthetic culture of our people. Some of the finest talent of the Public Platform of to-day have spoken in Memorial Hall.

The Post Office.

Up to the year 1864, all the mail for Springville came to Royer's Ford, and it was then brought over to this side of the river by some one, and delivered to the people, from the stores. But in this year a petition, largely signed, praying for a post office, and that Mr. John Sheeler who then had a store in the building now occupied by the bicycle works at the west end of the canal bridge, be appointed as postmaster, was forwarded to Washington. The petition was granted, and Mr. Sheeler's commission dated from November of that year. "East Vincent" was the name of the office, at first, but in 1872 the name was changed to Spring City. One mail a day each way was at first distributed, and the postmaster received about One Hundred Dollars a year for carrying and distributing the mail.

This is the list of postmasters thus far. The date after every one shows the time of his commission:—

John Sheeler, November, 1864; D. S. Taylor, May, 1867; J. G. Yeager, July, 1867; D. S. Taylor, March, 1869; Dr. W. P. Snyder, October, 1883; Walter Macfeat, July, 1885, D. M. Curry, February, 1890; Jacob Leidy, February, 1895; G. Clinton Williams, March, 1899.

The office was in the fourth-class until July, 1891. Since 1891 it is a third-class office, and the postmasters are now appointed by the President of the United States, and confirmed by the Senate.

THE PUBLIC SCHOOLS.

The first public school was held in the Lyceum, and for several years this was the only place in the village where pupils were trained. About the year 1849 the school was transferred to the basement of Union Meeting House, and here it remained until about 1857, when the first public school-house was built. Some of those who taught in the Union Meeting House were Jacob Latshaw, John Funk, Albert Simpson, and Lindley Frankum.

The first building erected solely for public school purposes, stood on Hall Street where the tenement houses, now belonging to the Lutheran Church, are. It lasted only a few years. In 1863 it was torn down and the stones and other materials were used in erecting another public school-house, which yet stands on the lot in the rear of the Lutheran parsonage. School was held here until 1872, when the school was transferred to the large building opposite the M. E. Church. In 1859 a school-house known as the "Western School," was built on West Bridge Street, which did service until 1880, when the school was transferred to the main building. In 1871 the beautiful school building, which is so frequently praised by visitors who come to our town, was erected.

PUBLIC SCHOOL BUILDING SPRING CITY

At first four rooms were provided. Then in 1881 the middle section of four rooms was added. In 1892 the rear section was built, consisting of two rooms on the first floor, and the High School room, class room, and philosophical room on the upper story.

The School Board which so wisely planned and provided for the school interests of the children was composed, in 1871, of Davis Hause, Esq., Dr. William Brower, Messrs. Thomas J. Coulston, Christian S. Lessig, David S. Taylor, and Jones Rogers. These principals have had charge of the educational training of the young thus far: Messrs. Joseph X. Smith, Adjalon R. Shantz, and Jacob K. Jones. The first graduating class of four bowed to an audience in the lecture room of the M. E. Church in 1881. An alumni association of eighty-nine thus far is the result of the sixteen classes which have completed the prescribed course of instruction. Twelve teachers are now guiding the young of our borough through the labyrinth of knowledge.

The present Board are: President, Dr. W. Brower; Secretary, William Sower; Treasurer, A. F. Tyson; J. I. Mowrey, George M. Diemer, John Latshaw, W. C. Taylor, Joseph P. Thomas, William T. Williams, Dr. J. C. Mewhinney, Rev. J. M. S. Isenberg, and John S. Witt. Dr. Brower has been a member of the School Board uninterruptedly since he was appointed to fill a vacancy, in the early part of the year 1869. He is now just closing his tenth consecutive term of three years, and he has again been chosen to serve another term. Most of this time he has filled the office of either secretary or president. His wise and judicious counsels have been given on every question of school interest during all these thirty years. This noble gentleman is also supposed now to have behind him the longest unbroken term of service of any school director in the county.

THE BOROUGH ORGANIZED.

In 1867 the borough was organized under the name of Springville, but in 1872 the name was changed to Spring City. The following is the list of Burgesses with the date of first election, when they served more than one term:—

David G. Wells.......1867; Joseph Johnson.......1868;
Casper S. Francis......1869; James H. Du Gan.....1871;
Charles Peters ....1872; David G. Wells........1874;
E. C. B. Shaner.......1875; Henry S. Stoll........1881;
E. C. B. Shaner.......1882; Joseph Keeley 1886;
Jones Diemer.........1889; William Sower........1890;
J. C. Mewhinney, M.D..1891; George D. Peters......1892;
J. Evans Yeager......1894; William Albright, Esq..1897.
Henry J. Diehl, 1899, by appointment.

NEWSPAPERS OF SPRING CITY.

The first newspaper, "The Iron Man," was printed by Mr. John E. Lewis, and was sent out as a monthly, four-paged sheet, in February, 1870. The paper was 12 by 18 inches in size, and 400 copies of it were sent out. The subscription price was to be seventy-five cents a year. "The Iron Man" made his visits at irregular intervals for several months when the project was dropped.

The next attempt at printing and circulating a local newspaper was made by Mr. John H. Royer, who, on March 27, 1872, sent out the first issue of "The Spring City Sun," a weekly sheet. This paper soon found an admission to 1300 homes weekly. Mr. Royer was the editor and proprietor until

DR. WILLIAM BROWER
PRESIDENT OF THE SCHOOL BOARD

May, 1887, when Messrs. Carney and Shull purchased the entire business from Mr. Royer, and they began using the composing stick. In September, 1895, Mr. Cornelius McKinsey purchased Mr. Shull's interest in the firm. Since then the paper, under the present management, finds its way into 1200 homes. The "Sun" is bright, crisp, and newsy.

THE NATIONAL BANK.

The National Bank of Spring City was chartered on April 20, 1872, with a cash capital of $100,000. The building, ground, safe, and bank fixtures cost about Eleven Thousand Dollars. The first Board of Directors was: Messrs. Casper S. Francis, Charles Peters, Benjamin Prizer, John R. Miller, A. D. Hunsicker, Charles Tyson, John Stauffer, Benjamin Rambo, and Jacob Christman. Mr. Casper S. Francis was its first president, and Mr. John T. Eaches was first cashier.

When the bank threw open its doors for business on Monday morning, September 25th, of the above year, a little rivalry occurred between Messrs. Joseph Johnson and William Priest as to who should make the first deposit of money. Mr. Johnson was the winner in the race, and made his appearance first at the window. He counted down *Three Hundred Dollars* as the first deposit at the bank, and gave the money to teller, William J. Wagoner.

STOCK.

In July, 1874, the capital stock of the bank was increased to $150,000, and in July, 1886, a further increase of $50,000 was made, thus swelling the amount to $200,000, the present working capital. National banks are required by law to set aside an amount equal to twenty per cent. of their capital

stock as a surplus fund. This bank has now complied fully
with the requirements of the act, and $40,000 are now in the
said fund.

The corporation has made for itself a good financial rec-
ord. Its stock has always sold well, and it has paid good
dividends. One of the solid financial institutions of our town
is the National Bank. The present Board of Directors is:
President, Mr. A. P. Fritz; Secretary, Dr. W. Brower; Milton
Latshaw, Franklin March, Esq., D. B. Latshaw, Davis Knauer,
Penrose Brownback, Edward Brownback, and C. W. Fryer.
Cashier, William J. Wagoner.

THE SPRING CITY CORNET BAND.

The first steps, looking toward the formation of this
superb musical organization, were taken at a preliminary
meeting held October 6, 1866, in Mr. Henry F. Caswell's tin
store on South Main Street, where Mr. Hosea Latshaw's bak-
ery now is. They met afterward in the school-house, now in
the rear of Lutheran parsonage. The date of organization
which is cited in the constitution is October 22, 1866. This
is the first list of officers: President, Franklin C. Buckwalter;
Secretary, William J. Wagoner; Treasurer, Mahlon Rogers.
The first musical instructor of the band was Mr. John G.
Moses, then leader of The Phœnixville Military Band, and
the first leader was Mr. Henry F. Caswell.

GOVERNMENT.

Messrs. H. F. Caswell and Martin Lapp, who had been
appointed for that purpose, drew up and presented a constitution and by-laws which the members of the band agreed
to respect and obey. The constitution has seventeen, and the
by-laws have thirty-eight well-defined articles of government

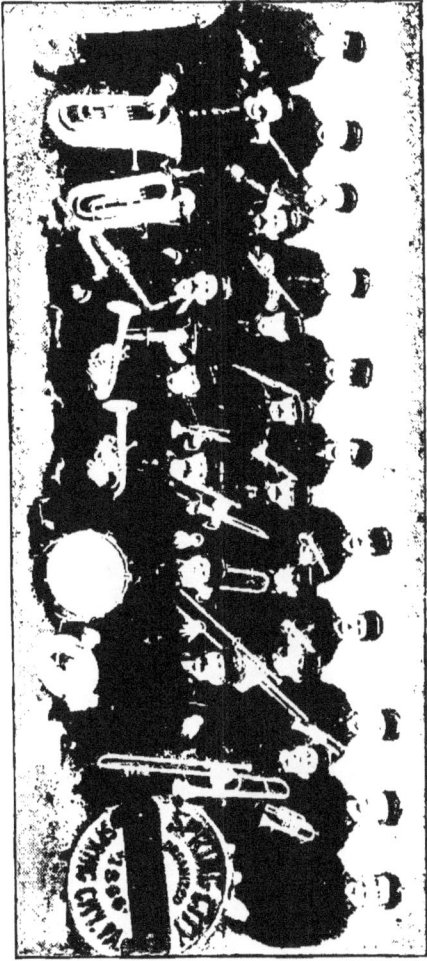

SPRING CITY CORNET BAND

suitable for the purpose. In a modified form they are still in good use.

OBJECT.

As shown by Article II of the constitution, the object of the organization is couched in these words: "The object of the Band shall be to acquire a knowledge of the art and science of music, and to make it a source of pleasure and refinement to ourselves and to the citizens of Springville and vicinity." This is a good aim.

DUES AND INITIATION.

In order to meet and defray the expenses of purchasing the instruments for the Band, a promissory note of Five Hundred Dollars was given, and signed by the members of the institution. The members then in the by-laws, taxed themselves two dollars each, a month, as a sinking fund with which to pay off the note. In addition to this, thirty-five cents a week each, were charged when the music teacher was present; and an additional five cents a week regular dues were charged. Ten dollars initiation were also charged. Afterward the initiation was made five dollars, and the dues ten cents a week. This is the custom now. The minutes show that Messrs. Francis Latschar, William J. Wagoner, Franklin C. Buckwalter, Ira Place, James Place, and Mahlon Rogers were the first members to pay the ten dollars initiation into the treasury. This they did in the order named.

NAME.

The Band has had three names. At a meeting held October 22, 1866, the name chosen was "The Perseverance Brass Band of Springville." May 12, 1868, the name was changed to "The Springville Cornet Band," and on June 4, 1872, the name of "The Spring City Cornet Band" was given to the institution, and ordered to be painted on the bass drum head. This name still holds.

INSTRUMENTS, WAGON, ETC.

The Band of 1866 had seventeen players in it. The instruments which were of brass, with the bell back, were purchased by their leader, Mr. J. G. Moses, from the Messrs. Stratton, of New York, at the cost of about $500. Three sets of instruments have been used by the Band, and now the fourth set is in use. These latter are known as the "Besson" instruments, and they were manufactured in London, England. They cost about Nine Hundred Dollars. Five sets of uniform have been used, at an average cost of about Seventeen Dollars per individual. During the thirty-two years of its existence, it has cost an average of about Five Hundred and Fifty Dollars a year to defray the expenses of the Band.

Up to the year 1868 no wagon was owned by the Band, but in that year a suitable wagon was purchased from the Messrs. Flemming and Gardner of Philadelphia, at a cost of about Six Hundred Dollars. This wagon was in use until 1884. When Mr. Leonard Mowrey's barn burned that year, the wagon which happened to be in the barn at the time, was also consumed. The present wagon, purchased in 1885 of Messrs. Langardt & Son of Philadelphia, cost Seven Hundred and Twenty-five Dollars.

THEIR DEBUT.

On July 4, 1867, the Band made their first appearance on the streets of the borough to play. On that day they marched from the band house down Main Street then back,

1595980

and across the river, and out to Mrs. Vanderslice's grove, near where Fernwood Cemetery now is. Here they spent the Fourth, dispensing music to their many friends. Their first paid engagements were on August 31, 1867, when they played for the American Mechanics in a parade, for Forty Dollars. They also received Twenty Dollars each for playing at the Sunday-School picnics of Garwood's and Hobson's Sunday-School that year.

LEADERS.

Since Mr. Moses laid down the baton as leader, these have followed: Messrs. Frank Beerbrower, John Fox, Isaac Kulp, William R. Brooke, August Augsburg, Aaron Eschelman, Stephen Schaeffer, and John C. Cummings its present leader. The member of longest standing in the Band is Mr. Isaac Kulp, who has played with the organization continually since 1871. Two of his sons, Howard and Willis, are also members of long standing.

THE PRESENT BAND.

The Band of to-day has twenty-two players. The degree of musical skill attained at the present time is hard to equal, and much harder to surpass. *Quality of tone*, and not noise, is their aim. Unstinted praise is lavished on them wherever they play. They compare well with the Ringgold and Germania bands of Reading. The solos rendered on the cornet, clarinet, saxophone, and baritone are exceedingly sweet. The free open-air concerts now given over the borough are much admired.

THE LIBERTY STEAM FIRE COMPANY, No. 1.

On July 9, 1881, just five days after the Shantz & Keeley Stove Works burned down, a meeting of the citizens of the borough was held in Mechanics' Hall with the object of forming some sort of organized effort to fight fires. A committee, composed of Messrs. D. S. Taylor, Charles Peters, Milton Latshaw, C. S. Lessig, and Samuel H. Egolf, was appointed to await on the Borough Council, and solicit their aid in the matter.

They appeared before the council, and made three requests of them:—

First.—That the Council should purchase a fire apparatus, and the citizens sustain them.

Second.—That the Council exonerate Mr. O. B. Keeley from tax for ten years, if he rebuild the foundry; and,

Third.—That the Council pay the expense of the fire engine in service at the late fire.

This they agreed to do.

THE ENGINE PURCHASED.

A committee, part councilmen and part citizens, purchased, January 28, 1882, from the Silsby Manufacturing Company, of Seneca Falls, New York, the Silsby fire engine and hose at a cost of Three Thousand Six Hundred Dollars. The committee was composed of Messrs. D. S. Taylor, Abel Wainwright, John Flemings, Andrew McMichael, and H. S. Francis.

The engine remained the property of the Borough Council until April 1, 1889. It was then purchased by The Liberty Steam Fire Engine Company, No. 1. together with the hose and equipments, for One Thousand Dollars. In the fall

LIBERTY STEAM FIRE ENGINE HOUSE, SPRING CITY

of 1896, a new boiler, wheels, springs, etc., were placed on the engine, at a cost of upwards of Two Thousand Dollars.

VOLUNTEER FIRE COMPANY.

For about ten years there was no definitely organized fire company; but, on January 9, 1882, a citizens' meeting was held in Mechanics' Hall with the object of forming a Volunteer Fire Company. A committee of five, of which Mr. II. J. Diehl was chairman, was appointed to procure names to organize said company. At a second meeting, January 16, 1882, H. T. Hallman was elected foreman; H. J. Diehl, assistant; and Messrs. John Ullman, Perry Setzler, Lewis Colwell, Zachariah Brinard, George Keim, Robert Berstler, Charles Tyson, and John Oberholtzler, were elected pipe men.

A constitution of sixteen articles and a by-law code of eighteen suitable articles for the government of such an organization were at once adopted.

ENGINE-HOUSES.

In the year 1881 the first engine-house, corner of Hall and Church Streets, was built by the Borough Council at a cost of about One Thousand Six Hundred Dollars. In the year 1890 the lot on Hall Street, 40 by 135 feet, on which the present engine-house stands, was secured, and on August 5, 1890, Messrs. George D. Peters, E. Derrick, Dr. W. P. Snyder, Calvin Snyder, and II. T. Hallman, were appointed as a building committee to have erected a suitable building into which to house the fire engine. The house and the ground on which it stands cost about Five Thousand Five Hundred Dollars. The building was dedicated on July 4, 1892, by a parade, and suitable other exercises.

MEMBERSHIP.

At first there were *Active*, *Honorary*, and *Contributing* members in the Company, all of whom paid One Dollar a year dues. Now the members are all styled *Active*, and fifty cents a year are collected as dues. The requirements for membership are that a person must be a citizen of Spring City, bear a good moral character, and be upwards of eighteen years of age. The consent of the parent or guardian is required of those between the age of eighteen and twenty-one years. Thirty members signed the constitution and by-laws as charter members, and thus far upwards of one hundred and eighty names have been enrolled, most of whom are in good standing.

The Company meets for business regularly on the first Tuesday evening of every month, and the officers are selected annually on the first Tuesday of January. Now, 1898, these persons are in charge of the meetings: President, P. H. Brower; Vice-president, Ambrose Keffer; Recording Secretary, W. E. Leighton; Financial Secretary, John F. Fry; Treasurer, William H. Rogers.

SERVICES.

This Company, like most volunteer companies, has always been very prompt in rendering every assistance within their power, in case of a conflagration. It matters not how the surroundings may be when the alarm is struck, the boys always flee to the rescue. Through Arctic cold, or torrid heat, day or night, the fire laddies always respond, and do their utmost to save property from the flames. They have behind them a record of faithful services. They are worthy of the financial support of our people. They thus far, in the sixteen years of their existence, have been present and battled against upwards of thirty fires.

THE SILSBY FIRE ENGINE

CHAPTER II.

FIRST PREACHING, 1845.

In the spring of the above year the sun came back as usual from his annual journey to the south, and poured his warm rays on the hundred or more people who lived then in Springville. These people had their houses scattered along Main Street. A good portion of the town was at that time covered with woods. Here the birds built their nests, sang their songs, reared their young unmolested, and were happy. Much of the territory now lying west of Main Street was then either farm land or covered with timber. In fact, much of the lumber which was used in building the first river bridge, had been cut from the land between Yost Avenue and New Street.

Then the road which led from the west end of the river bridge, proceeded as now, across the canal, then down Main Street to the foot of Hall Street. Here it turned up Hall Street, then wound around the corner at Church Street, and led out by the Lutheran parsonage, then out to the Schuylkill Road to what was then known as "Kimes' Hotel." South Main Street was not opened for travel for several years afterward. When the borough was laid out, these old road-ways served as street lines, and this accounts for the fact that these streets are not more nearly straight.

This was the Springville of 1845. At this time the Methodist Episcopal Church hereabouts had preaching stations at Evansburg, 1835; Coventryville, 1774; Ebenezer, 1831

(?); Phœnixville, 1826; Valley Forge, 1831; Pottstown, 1836; Temple, 1840; St. John's, 1843, and Bethel, 1844.

Up to this time no effort seems to have been put forth here to sow the seeds of Gospel truth in the heart of man. But one beautiful Sabbath afternoon, after preaching at Bethel Church, the Rev. Peter J. Cox came here by invitation of Mr. David Wells, a member of Bethel Church, and preached in the evening in the Lyceum *the first sermon ever preached in Springville.* The Rev. Mr. Cox, then twenty-six years old, was a Junior Methodist preacher on the Pottstown circuit, under Rev. John Shields as Senior. Afterward he became a Presiding Elder of the same district.

When it was announced among the good people of the village that there were to be preaching services in the Lyceum, a desire at once prompted the people to hear the young man. So they came, and when the minister arose to announce the first hymn, he held a small group of hearers before him. They listened earnestly to the Word of God. No one living can tell how the few men, women, and children, who came to hear that first sermon from a young man with trembling knees, were impressed. We cannot say how deep were the convictions upon souls that were not much accustomed to placing themselves under the influence of the Gospel. But the Truth was received, at least, kindly: for at the close of the sermon, the Rev. Mr. Cox was earnestly invited to come and preach again. He came again. Others came, and as time went on, preaching services were more frequent.

PREACHING CONTINUED.

Thus, while Generals Taylor and Scott were carrying the United States stars and stripes into Mexican soil, and driving the hordes of General Santa Anna back, thus widening the

borders of our beloved country, the good people of Springville took their first steps toward planting the banner of King
Immanuel on the banks of the classic Schuylkill. Now began
the means of driving back the works of sin and Satan here.
Preaching services were continued in the Lyceum mostly by
the Junior Ministers of the church for about six years, or
during the most of the first decade. As time rolled on the
membership hereabouts began to increase, then religious
services became more frequent. In fact, such services became
a necessity. They grew in interest and power as might be
expected. Frequently after an afternoon service at Bethel
a few of the members there would accompany the minister
to Springville to help him sing at an evening service, in the
Lyceum. Short prayer meetings were often held after preaching, and these same meetings were frequently inspired and
enlivened by an experience meeting. In this and other ways,
the necessity of church membership and holy living were, in
a practical way, impressed on those who had not yet seen
their way to their Saviour. It was a personal knowledge of
a personal Redeemer that these pioneer Methodists were urg-
ing on their unconverted neighbors and friends. They taught
that Jesus Christ has power on earth to forgive sins, and that
the persons whose sins are thus forgiven, will assuredly know
this fact by the indwelling of God's Holy Spirit.

THE JUNIOR PREACHERS.

Who were these Junior preachers? Some of my young
readers may be interested in knowing something about them.
They surely were a very valuable adjunct in pushing forward
the work of soul-saving in their day. Well, they were young,
single men who had shown a disposition in their own home
church to work for God. Whereupon the Quarterly Confer-

ence of their home church recommended them as fit persons to be licensed for preaching. The Presiding Elder of their district then gave them a Local Preacher's License, and put them to work. Soon they joined the Annual Conference. Here they were appointed and sent to work on a district under the direction of the Senior preacher. The Senior preacher generally preached every four weeks at a charge. He always managed to be present and administer the Emblems on sacramental day.

These young men full of vim and of spiritual energy, were ready to do anything in their power to further the work of their Master in whom they had abiding faith. They generally boarded around in the families of the church members. In this way they were enabled to preach at different charges. For their services they were allowed the snug little sum of *One Hundred Dollars* a year. Young man, things have changed in the church during the last fifty years, as well as in the State. As soon as one of these Juniors succeeded in taking to himself a wife, he was transferred to take charge of a district or a charge for himself.

CLOSE OF SERVICES AT THE LYCEUM.

Several attempts at holding revivals were made in the Lyceum. In connection with the other preachers we must not forget to mention the valuable services of Rev. G. A. Shryock, a local preacher and foreman at the Paper Mill, who assisted in revival work at this time. Several persons were converted at the Lyceum. Some of the reliable material of the church commenced the service of God in this strange church. Mr. John Garber, father of Mr. Uriah Garber, who is now a member of the Trustee Board, was the first person converted here.

The little Christian band thus labored on, trusting always for greater results. Services continued. Sometimes they were held on Sabbath afternoon or in the evenings just as a preacher could be obtained. In the year 1851 they bid adieu to the Lyceum, and they then held services in the New Union Meeting House. For six years, at various times, the Word of God had been proclaimed in the Lyceum. The good seed of redemptive salvation had been sown. The pioneers have done the best that they could. The Lyceum is now growing too small to accommodate the increasing congregations which come to hear the Life-giving Word. Why not hold services in the Union Meeting House? It is now about finished. All agree to have the next services in the new church. But before leaving, let us write the inscription "*Well Done*" on the labors thus far.

CHAPTER III.

THE UNION MEETING HOUSE ERECTED.

The winter of 1847-48 found the carpenters employed by Mr. Jacob Sheeder, busy at work in an old stone barn which stood where Mr. Charles Peter's house now is, at the corner of Chestnut and Church Streets. On the floor of this barn the window and door frames, doors, window-sash, and other necessary materials were "worked out" by hand for a new meeting house to be built in Springville. The heavy outside doors were made by Mr. E. C. B. Shaner, yet living (1899).

During the summer of 1848 Mr. James Rogers, Sr., who was a wide awake, public-spirited gentleman, together with Messrs. Jesse Finkbiner, Amos Gearhart, and others, had a suitable building erected for religious purposes. The building was of stone, plastered on the outside, two stories high, and it was 40 by 60 feet in size, and cost about One Thousand One Hundred and Twenty Dollars. The structure was known as "The Union Meeting House." In this building could be held religious services of all denominations, if the people so desired.

DESCRIPTION.

Unfortunately no photograph of the building was ever taken; but an effort has been made to reproduce it from memory. This, perhaps, looks somewhat like the building, which stood on the site now occupied by the present church, and which extended east and west. The entrance was at the

THE UNION MEETING HOUSE OF 1855

east end. Two flights of steps, one from each side, led up to·
an outside platform, as shown in the drawing. Two doors led·
from the platform into an audience room which seated about
250 people. Two windows were in the west end, or end next
to what is now Church Street. The date board in the east
gable bore the date 1848.

Church Street was not then opened. In order to come
to the church people came up Hall Street to where the M. E..
parsonage now stands. Then they turned from the road and
drove or walked through an open lot now occupied by the
parsonage, then through the parsonage lot, and entered the
church lot near where the sheds now stand.

At this time all that portion now occupied by Church
Street, the public school property and thereabouts was embraced as farm land. Hence it was open fields. A picket
fence extended up along the line of Church Street, back of
the old church, possibly along where the pavement now is.
Through this fence, which always had a couple of pickets off,
the boys who came from the west side could easily go on
their way to church.

BURYING GROUND.

It was the custom then, as it is now, to bury the dead
near the place of public worship. In this way people could
visit the places of their departed loved ones, drop a bouquet
over the remains, and at the same time attend church. So
it was about the old Union Church. In the ground about
the east end of the church, about a dozen or fifteen graves
had been dug.

The church parlor-extension now rests on ground which
at one time was occupied by some of these graves. One grave,
that of a drowned boatman, was placed alongside the church

near the west end. Mr. James Rogers, Sr., wife and some of their grandchildren, were deposited here. In 1872 the bodies were removed and deposited in other places, mostly at Bethel and at the East Vincent burying ground.

INSIDE THE BUILDING.

Let us open one of the heavy doors leading from the platform, enter the building, look around, and observe how it looked. An aisle led from each door through the building to the west end. A row of seats six feet long extended from each aisle to the wall. The space between the aisles, the body of the church, was occupied by long seats with a division through the centre of them. Men and women in those days did not sit together. So here the same custom prevailed. The ladies entered the door leading from the north end of the platform, and so they occupied the north side of the room. The gentlemen entered by the other door, and so they were seated on the south side of the room.

The pulpit was at the west end of the room. When the minister stood up before his congregation to preach, the ladies were on his left, and the opposite sex, on his right side. Thus you notice the inside arrangements were just the opposite to what they now are.

The choir occupied a place in the middle block of seats in the rear, just inside and between the doors. At first the singers sat on a level with the other part of the congregation; but afterward the floor where they sat was elevated so as to give a better effect to the singing. It was here that the first choir, under the direction of Mr. George K. Hoffman, sat, and stimulated the worshiping audience with their hymn singing.

BASEMENT.

The basement story did not occupy the entire space within the walls. The entrance door, as you may see, was under the platform. The end next to Church Street was under ground, and it was not occupied. But the eastern end of the room was fitted up at once for school-room purposes, and it was rented to the East Vincent School Board for that use.

A continuous pine desk extended around the walls of the room, as was the custom in those days; so that when the pupils were seated at their desks, their backs were turned to the teacher, and their faces to the wall.

Some time after the public and private schools had been removed from this basement room, the Trustees of the church fitted it up suitable for a dwelling, in which the church sextons could reside. From the entrance door under the platform, there was a hall which led through the centre of the basement. On each side of the hall there was a room entered by a door from the hall. The apartment on the left or south side of the hall was the kitchen. On the north side of the hall was the parlor. Back of the kitchen there was a sleeping room. Back of the parlor there was a general stow-away place retained by the church for its own use.

Here in these three rooms, kitchen, parlor, and sleeping room, during the latter years of the Union Meeting House's existence, lived the sextons. The first to live here was Mr. John H. Setzler, one year, 1867 to 1868. Then Mr. George S. Sheffy, 1868 to 1871, and Mr. William Hoffman who died there. His wife remained there until the church was razed in 1872. The sextons lived rent free, with the exception of Mr. Sheffy, who paid a small rent. For the rent, the sextons cared for the church.

FINISHING OF THE CHURCH.

The upper room of the church was not finished for some time after it had been built. For we find that after Mr. James Rogers, Sr., in 1851, secured the property at sheriff sale he immediately employed his carpenter, Mr. Jacob Sheeder, to make and put in place the pulpit and the seating capacity. Mr. Rogers was careful to instruct Mr. Sheeder "not to put too much work or expense on it." Mr. Rogers' plans were carefully carried out. The pulpit and the pews were all made of pine wood, by hand, and in accordance with the style of church furnishing of that day. The furniture was all painted white.

No cellar heaters were in this church, nor were there any beautiful banks of bronzed steam radiators to distribute heat to the room. But two, large coal stoves of the Morning Light pattern, one on each side of the room, changed the chilly atmosphere and made it comfortable. These did their work well; for we are told that at times it was very warm in the room, especially when demonstrations of excitement marked the proceedings.

IN THE NEW CHURCH.

Happy were the people of the village when, in 1851, the New Union Meeting House was finished and declared open for holding religious services. As yet no religious denomination was strong enough in Springville to band themselves together and start a preaching station or mission for holding services in their own faith. Hence the wisdom and good fraternal feeling which existed to a greater or less extent among the people at large, prompted this "Union" enterprise. It is only one out of a thousand similar instances all over the land where the Lord directs his people to take the proper steps for planting his church of the different denominations among his chil-

dren. And He always succeeds, for "where the spirit of the
Lord is, there is liberty." 2 Cor. 3:17.

In the present case it seemed that the Methodists obtained the lead from the start in providing facilities for religious worship in our quiet little borough. At times not only
the preachers, but also members from Phœnixville and other
places drove here in groups, and helped to conduct a good,
pointed religious service. •

Thus the work continued for four years yet in the new
church before the end of the first decade. The interest increased, the influence widened until the year 1855. In this
way an audience would always greet the minister, and his
efforts at expounding the Word would be helped by the faith-
freighted prayers of those before him. But now the time is
at hand for the dozen or more Christians here to band themselves together under the name of a church organization.
They talk the matter over. They pray over it. They trust
that the Lord will help them, if they are willing to do their
part. Yes; they are willing, and they are in earnest. A committee is appointed to wait on Mr. James Rogers, Sr., and to
negotiate for the purchase of the Union Meeting House property. This committee carried out their mission, as will be
cited further on in our narrative. They were now regularly
appointed by the Quarterly Conference as Trustees, and au-
thorized to purchase a suitable place in which to hold services.
They were also personally assured by the Rev. Abram Freed,
the preacher in charge of this district at that time, that
Springville would be made a regular appointment.

Thus ends our first decade. Ten years have now elapsed
since the first Gospel sound was struck here. The people
have done their best. Now, in placing the bolt over the gate
which closes this first division of our narrative, we shall seal
it with the word *Success.*

CHAPTER IV.

TITLE TO THE PROPERTY.

The land now in possession of the Trustees of the M. E. Church, and on which the parsonage and the church are located, was orignally in two tracts. The first of these embraced the ground occupied by the parsonage, and the deeds show that it embraced "one-fourth of an acre of land." The second tract adjoined the first, and contained "forty-three and one-half square perches of land"; and, as the deed shows, "the second being the same whence the Union Meeting House now stands." The whole tract as embraced in the last deed given, covers an area of "eighty-three and one-half square perches of land."

As shown by the records, in the year 1842 a Mr. John Cox and his wife, for the consideration of *Fifty Dollars*, executed a deed to Mr. James Rogers, Sr., covering the first of these tracts. The second tract was deeded about the same time by Mr. Joseph Sowers and Maria, his wife, and Mr. Gideon Weikel and his wife, also to Mr. James Rogers, Sr., each for a like consideration, making One Hundred and Fifty Dollars for the entire ground.

As already cited, in 1848 Mr. Rogers and others built the Union Church on this tract of land. The financial outcome of the enterprise was not as good as it was expected. So the undertaking struggled along during the next three years with the signs of success sometimes encouraging, sometimes otherwise, until in 1851. On January 30th of this year, Mr. Davis Bishop, at that time high sheriff of Chester County, sold the entire church property at sheriff's sale to Mr. Rogers, who held the greater part of the lien against it.

TITLE TRANSFERRED TO THE METHODISTS.

Mr. Rogers now held the title to the property until April 11, 1855, when he and his wife Mary, in consideration of *Eleven Hundred and Twenty-five Dollars*, did execute the deed now in possession of the trustees of the church, to David Wells, Henry Prizer, John Finkbiner, David Longacre, and Thomas Bechtel, and their successors, "trustees in trust; that they hold such meeting house and premises for the use of the members of the Methodist Episcopal Church in the United States of America, according to the rules and discipline which, from time to time may be agreed upon, and adopted by the ministers and preachers of the said church at their general conferences." "And, in further trust and confidence, that they shall, at all times forever hereafter, permit such ministers and preachers belonging to said church, to preach and expound God's Holy Word therein."

It will be noticed from the above quotations taken from the deed, that great pains had been taken to enumerate the specific uses for which the property was conveyed. All the conveyances of title up to this deed of 1855, merely conveyed the title, with no special reference mentioned as to what use was to be made of the property. Now, the transfer is made "for the ministers and preachers of the Methodist Episcopal Church to preach and expound God's Holy Word." It is here clearly shown that, while Mr. Rogers and his wife were willing to transfer the title, they still wished that the Word of God should be proclaimed to the people of Springville. This shows their wise foresight.

Again, another very strong incentive thrown out at this
time for the propagation of the Gospel here was, that Mr.
Rogers required two of the leading trustees already mentioned,
Messrs. John Finkbiner and David Wells, to give their "joint
and several" promissory note to secure the payment of the
sum enumerated in the deed.

This was a critical period for the pioneer Methodists.
They now were to assume the duties and responsibilities of
establishing a preaching station here where some of them had
thus far spent their lives. When they enumerated their forces,
they could count only about *twelve active members* who constituted the Springville Methodist Episcopal Church at the
beginning of its career. But soon a revival broke out which
swelled the ranks nicely.

A NEW ERA.

The Methodists were now fairly established. Preaching
services were held every Sabbath, and prayer meetings were
conducted on Wednesday evenings. Revival services were
conducted every year as before. The church began to take
on new strength, both in spiritual power and in numbers.
This is shown very clearly in Mr. Reuben Davis' class-book;
for, in January, 1858, he had the names of twenty members
enrolled, who were marked as "probationers." These and
others who did not join the Methodist Church were the result
of a revival held in the fall of 1857 by Rev. Joseph Dare.
The revival history and the strength of the church will be
more fully noticed in another place.

FINIS. UNION MEETING HOUSE.

We have now sketched briefly the history of the Union
Meeting House. It has sheltered God's people for twenty-

four years, and during seventeen of these years, its walls have reverberated the joyous outbursts of the happy Methodists. But, like all things earthly, this first home of John Wesley's followers here must have an end. The financial indebtedness which had hung so heavily on the shoulders of the members in 1855 was, in the year 1868, all paid, and the church property was free from such encumbrance.

As the Lyceum had grown too small for church services, so now, 1872, the people were again cramped for room. This was especially the case during revival services. To use the language of one of the ministers of that time, "The aisles were crowded, and I could see the carriage whips in the hands of men dangling over the heads of the people who were compelled to stand during service, or perhaps, to sit in the windows."

In March, 1872, the Rev. John H. Wood was assigned to this place as pastor. While going up the rickety steps leading to the platform for entering the church to preach on the evening of the first day, his foot caught and he made a misstep. This nearly caused an accident to the gentleman. While in the pulpit that evening the reverend gentleman took the occasion to remark, "It is time to build a new church before somebody gets his neck broken."

The subject of a new church was then the great topic which was discussed by the sixty members in good standing then enrolled. Some favored; some were slow to take hold of the proposed new church project. Many were the regrets among the members at seeing the old structure removed. Indeed, there is something solemn, something reverential about a building which has been dedicated to the use and service of Almighty God. And the feeling of reverential awe seems to deepen with age. It grows on us so slowly, so quietly, and yet so surely. Then when such a sacred structure in which God has so often visited his people in the plentitude of his mercy and grace, is to pass from sight, emotions arise in the soul which are almost ineffable. Memory loves to muse around the old hallowed landmark. In short, we are loath to part with a treasure which lies so closely to the tendrils of our affections.

Well, it was so; at least, with the Old Union Meeting House. Some of the members of the church who were so closely joined to this almost hallowed spot, could not lay a hand on the precious building now to help demolish it. To them it had been, and still was, a blessed spot. And why not? It was within those sacred walls that many of them were born into God's holy family. It was around that old-fashioned, sharp-cornered, rectangular shaped altar that they had so often knelt to partake of the emblems of our "Saviour's broken body and shed blood." And, as they did so, how often they felt the rekindlings of that heaven-born spirit of love which had been planted in their hearts' affections when God, for Christ's sake, pardoned their sin! Fathers and mothers had not seen any of their sons and daughters united in the bonds of Holy matrimony here, for there never had been any church weddings solemnized in the Union Meeting House. But they had seen here many of their offspring joined to the Heavenly Bride, the church which our Saviour purchased with his own precious blood. And that was still better. Then, oh the sweeping revivals which had been held on this spot! These retrospective glances at things past were too much; too affecting for some of the membership.

But the onward move of God's work demands that the past and the present must give place to the future. The church must come down, and a larger and more commodious one must take its place.

Sunday morning, July 14th, dawned bright and beautiful. Rev. Wood preached to a good-sized audience, both morning and evening. The service of that day was the last service held in the old church. The audience now go down the rickety steps for the last time.

Adieu, Union Meeting House! On Monday morning the men climbed the roof of the building and sawed the same into four sections, and took them down carefully. Then the walls were soon removed, and the Old Union Meeting House which had served its mission so well, was no more.

CHAPTER V.

PREPARATIONS.

One morning the Rev. Mr. J. H. Wood met Mr. John Finkbiner under the overshoot of his barn, and there a business conversation ensued in reference to building a new church. The result was this: They agreed that Mr. Finkbiner should donate *One Thousand Dollars* to the project on condition that the Rev. Mr. Wood should raise *Three Thousand Dollars* additional. This was, at that time, considered to be a sum sufficiently large to erect a building of the size and style desired. It was found, however, by the time the church was finished, that it had cost *Eight Thousand*, instead of Four Thousand Dollars.

Under the direction of Messrs. Samuel Gracey, F. R. Guss, Allen Rogers, Simon Keim, and Jacob Keiter, as a building committee, the work of removing the old building and of erecting a new one was consummated.

A NEW BUILDING ERECTED.

At once work was commenced. The foundations of the present building, which is 80 by 45 feet, were soon laid. On Saturday, September 7, 1872, the corner-stone of the new building was laid. The Revs. Thomas Kirkpatrick and Thomas J. Fernley were present at the ceremony, the latter making the address to a good-sized crowd of people. There was no corner-stone in the old church; but when the present structure is taken down these things, among others, will be found in the corner-stone: several different coins, the names

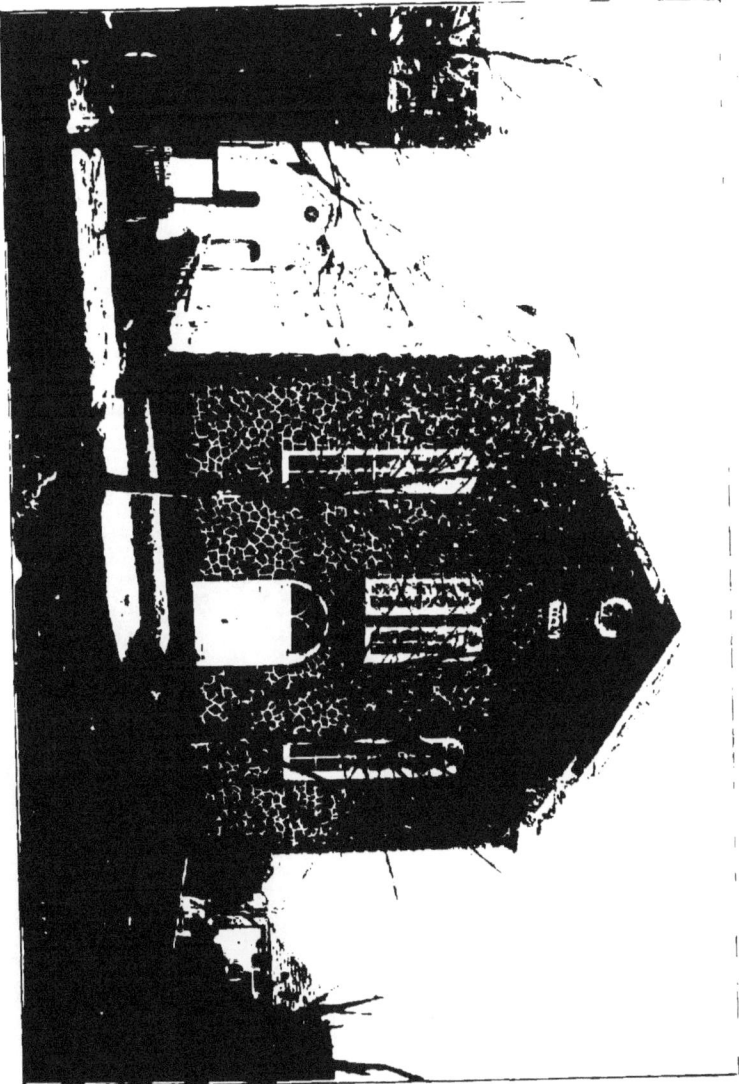

SPRING CITY METHODIST EPISCOPAL CHURCH

of the trustees and of the building committee, a copy of the Bible, a copy of the Spring City newspaper, all in a carefully closed tin box.

Messrs. Perry Mock and William Wyand did the beautiful rubble work in the front wall.

Owing to the lateness of the season in which the work was commenced, and to the extra labor required on the front wall; also, to the fact the horses hereabouts nearly all had the peculiar disease called "Epizooty," and, therefore, the material for the building could not be hauled, the building was not finished before the spring of 1873. As soon as the weather permitted in the spring, work was commenced and pushed forward rapidly. Lack of means prevented the completion of the structure at that time. The lower story only was completed.

DEDICATION.

While the new church was building, the congregation worshiped in the basement of Mechanics' Hall. Here, from July 14, 1872, to July 6, 1873, all the public services of the church had been held, except some of the prayer meetings, which were held at the parsonage. But the new building was now so nearly completed that on July 6, 1873, it was ready for dedication. This was a gala day at the church. The weather, which had been previously very warm, was much cooler on the above day. A large congregation filled the lecture room to enjoy a good day's worship, and they had a helpful time.

At 10 o'clock in the morning the Rev. S. H. C. Smith, of Tabernacle Church, Philadelphia, preached a fine sermon from Romans 12:11, and Rev. C. I. Thompson of Phœnixville, presented the subject of finances. In the afternoon the

Rev. Thompson preached a "good, stirring sermon," and again pressed the financial question. In the evening the Rev. George S. Broadbent, of Roxborough, Philadelphia, preached a sermon full of unction from Acts 9:17.

The dedicatory services were performed by Rev. Broadbent immediately following the evening services. Thus the lecture room, at least, was dedicated as per the Book of Discipline, "as a Church for the service and worship of Almighty God."

Including Five Hundred Dollars contributed by the Ladies' Aid Society, the subscriptions for the day amounted to *Two Thousand One Hundred and Thirty-four Dollars.*

THE CHURCH FINISHED.

For six years, 1873 to 1879, the public services were all held in the lecture room. But during the winter of 1878-9 the church had been visited with a large revival, and a good harvest of souls was gathered to the Lord. In the spring of 1879 when the Rev. Joseph B. Graff came to take charge of the flock, he found that the time had now arrived for the completion of the church. The lower room was not large enough to accommodate the immense audiences which came to hear the Word.

We quote these words from the historical record of the church, at that time written by Rev. J. B. Graff: "The ingathering from the revival made larger church accommodations not only possible, but necessary. Therefore, in the early summer of 1879 the following named brethren were appointed as a building committee to overlook the completion of the main audience room of the church: John Sheeler, John Finkbiner, Allen Rogers, Samuel B. Latshaw, and Jesse G. Yeager. The work was completed under their direction, at a cost of

Two Thousand Five Hundred Dollars, and the room was dedicated to the worship of God on Sabbath, December 21, 1879. The following named brethren were present and participated in the dedicatory services: Revs. H. W. Warren (afterward bishop), G. D. Carrow, D.D., T. A. Fernley, J. H. Wood, Eli Pickersgill, George W. Lybrand; also, Maxwell S. Rowland of the Reformed Church." The cost of the improvements was all provided for at that time.

FRESCOING.

In the summer of 1886, Rev. N. D. McComas pastor, the lecture room of the church was frescoed at a cost of One Hundred and Twenty-five Dollars. The Ladies' Aid Society paid One Hundred and Fifteen Dollars of this bill, and the Sunday-School paid the balance.

The upper room had been frescoed when it was finished, but in 1896, Rev. D. M. Gordon pastor, it was again frescoed and painted. New carpet and new pulpit furniture were also supplied at this time. The Annex was also frescoed at this time. The entire cost of these improvements was One Thousand One Hundred and Thirty-six Dollars and Seventy-five Cents.

THE ANNEX.

Soon the Sunday-School grew too large to be accommodated in the lecture room; hence we find that, at the meeting of the Board of Trustees in June, 1884, a building committee, composed of Messrs. M. F. Sheeler, J. G. Yeager, and J. R. Weikel, was appointed to fix up a room in the basement of the church for the Infant Sunday-School. They at once proceeded to their task and had the room fixed up and furnished at a cost of about One Hundred and Fifty Dollars.

This served as the Infant Room until they moved into the basement of the Annex building in 1892.

At a meeting of the Trustee Board, held May 9, 1891, the contract to build the Annex, which now stands at the rear of the church, was awarded to Mr. Henry Spotts for Two Thousand Two Hundred and Twenty Dollars, he being the lowest bidder. The work was done under the supervision of this building committee: Messrs J. G. Yeager, J. A. Keiter, and Joseph A. Benjamin. The Annex, familiarly known as "The Parlor," is 31 feet 6 inches by 30 feet 6 inches in size, and two stories high. It was finished and opened for use in 1892. The total cost of the building and the contents was about Two Thousand Six Hundred Dollars.

The Infant Sunday-School now occupies the basement story of this building, and the advanced Sunday-School Bible classes occupy the upper room. Prayer meetings and spiritual class meetings are also held occasionally in the upper room.

STEWARDS OF SPRING CITY M. E. CHURCH

CHAPTER VI.

REVIVALS.

"Except a man be born again, he cannot see the kingdom of God." John 3: 3.

The Methodist Episcopal Church is nothing if she is not a revival church. She was born in a revival. As soon as she gives up the revival effort, her power is gone. The present strength and ability of the church in Spring City is due to the fact that the members have always been very zealous and persistent in revival work.

The revival history here, if carefully written out, would of itself form material enough for a fair-sized volume. Only a few of the more noted ingatherings can be here recorded. It is worthy of remembrance at this point to say, that when the people of God in Springville launched out and threw themselves on his promises, he sent the revival tide at just the right time, thus confirming the truth contained in Acts 2:47: "And the Lord added to the church daily such as should be saved."

During the time when services were held in the Lyceum, no very marked revivals are recorded. Special efforts were held every year, and some souls were converted; but nothing of special note resulted until the second year after the Union Meeting House came into possession of the Methodists. Hence we note first, the

REVIVAL OF 1857-8.

At the beginning of this epoch, 1855, there were about twelve members, all told, whose names were on the books.

These went to work earnestly, beseeching God to pour out
His spirit on the church, and this he did. During the fall
and winter of the above year, when Rev. Joseph Dare was in
charge, a marked revival broke out. The pastor at this time
lived at Phœnixville, and came up to attend to the work.
He was ably assisted by the Junior preacher, Rev. N. W.
Bennum. As the result of their labors, and of the lay members as well, about fifty persons professed conversion at that
time. Rev. Dare is yet very favorably remembered by some
of the older people hereabouts, as a man of great social quali-
ties. His sermons may not have been so full of doctrinal
theology, but they were scriptural, earnest, and convincing.
He went about among the people always wearing a smile and
giving a kind word of encouragement to them. He prayed
with the people and invited them to come to church. They
came and were benefited. What a wonderful help to the
church was this revival. Some of those converted at this
revival were: Samuel Gracey, John Gracey, Peter Grubb, Mrs.
Mary A. Taylor, Hannah Miller, and Mrs. Mary A. Sheeder.

REVIVAL OF 1860-1.

This revival dates the year in which the Rebellion broke
out. Just three years after the above revival, another out-
pouring came. This time Rev. J. B. Dennison was the
preacher in charge, and he was assisted by Rev. Isaac Mast
as Junior preacher. This was known as "The Dennison Revival." While the North and the South were lining up for
the Great Civil War of our nation, God's people here were
marshaling their forces against the army of Satan. The result of the former war was the liberating of *Three Millions*
of slaves. The Methodists took the Captain of their Salvation as their Leader, and forty or fifty souls claimed that they

had been liberated from the bondage of sin, in this revival. The army of the Lord was again greatly increased. Some of the trophies of this conquest were: William A. Weigel, Jonathan Priest, and Hon. Willis Bland (since law Judge of the Berks County Courts).

REVIVAL OF 1866-7.

The third marked increase to the church seems to have come during the above winter. Rev. John Allen was the preacher in charge at this time; but his assistant preacher, Rev. Adam L. Wilson, did most of the preaching and exhorting here. This was because revivals were in progress all over the circuit at nearly the same time; hence the Senior preacher could not be at any one station for a great length of time. Indeed, this was also the case in the other revivals. About thirty or thirty-five persons professed a change of heart at Springville this winter.

During this winter the revival tide broke out all over the circuit with a more or less marked degree of fervor. This is shown from the fact that, at the Quarterly Conference held at Coventry, January 5, 1867, just in the midst of the revival season, the pastor reported that he had taken into the church these members: Pottstown, 153; Bethel, 12; Springville, 20; Coventry, 18; and Ebenezer, 5. Here are a few of the names of persons who came into the light of salvation at this time: Allen Rogers, David R. Smith, John H. Setzler, George S. Sheffy, Annie Brownback, Mary M. Clemens, and Hannah J. Mills.

REVIVAL OF 1868-9.

We note as the fourth of the special ingatherings, the one which was held during the above-named winter. Rev.

Jacob P. Miller, pastor in charge. This revival followed immediately after the separation from the Coventryville Circuit. In the spring of 1868 Bethel and Springville were united under the name of "The Springville and Bethel Circuit." That winter the revival spirit struck both charges with about equal sway, for the result, as handed down to us is, that there were 101 souls who professed a change of heart at Bethel, and 100 at Springville. The meetings were characterized with wonderful solemnity. The Holy Spirit did his work well. The church was greatly quickened. In January, 1869, while the meetings were still in progress, the pastor reported to the Quarterly Conference that sixty had joined the church at Springville on probation, and sixty-five at Bethel. Among the probationers we find these names at that time: J. A. Guss, Simeon Keim, Willis Hunter, Maggie S. Brownback, Susan Shick, and Mrs. Kate V.-Gracey-Custer.

REVIVAL OF 1871-2.

Special revival number five, Rev. Richard Turner, pastor in charge, has a peculiar history. The pastor had held a revival in the fall at Springville, with apparently very little success. He then opened and proceeded to hold a series of special meetings at Bethel. But seed had been sown at Springville which was yet to bear fruit, for the Lord had so ordered. Some of the members here were still holding on to the Lord and pleading for a revival. The revival came. It broke out in the Sunday-School. One day while Mr. F. R. Guss was teaching school at the West Bridge Street school building, he noticed that a couple of the large school girls seemed to wear a sad expression. He inquired of them what was the matter. One of them replied, "Oh nothing!" and so the matter seemed to rest for that time. But before evening came, a note was laid on the teacher's desk by one of the girls, stating that there was something the matter with her. She stated that she felt she ought to have religion.

The teacher, that evening, communicated the good news to some of the church members. The girls were then invited to come to prayer meeting on the following Wednesday evening, and go to the altar to seek salvation. This they did. They were converted. Now the meetings were continued, and the spiritual zeal thus broken out anew, lasted all winter and into the next conference year. The succeeding pastor, Rev. J. H. Wood, told the writer that, when he came here in March, the meeting was going on "in full blast." Forty or fifty souls professed that their sins had been blotted out during this winter.

Nearly all of the preaching and exhorting during this precious season of refreshing and ingathering, had been done by Messrs. F. R. Guss, Samuel Gracey, and Simeon Keim, in the absence of the preacher in charge.

Some of the persons saved to the Lord in this effort were: Mrs. Alice-Rogers-Latshaw, Annie Wismer, Flora Lessig, Mrs. Rachel-Peters-Oliver, John A. Weigel, Jacob Elliott, Abraham Hallman, and Mrs. Melvina Hallman.

This was the last revival held in the Old Union Church. It looks as though God had especially blessed his people, through these years, so that they might be able to provide for him a more suitable place of worship. At least, this is what was done at this period of our history. How appropriate that the last revival held in the Old Union Meeting House should be such a glorious affair. No wonder that some of the church members were so unwilling to see the "Old Landmark" removed.

REVIVAL OF 1876-7.

Rev. Eli Pickergill was the preacher in charge when the sixth of the marked church quickenings took place. Between fifty and sixty is the number handed down to us as this winter's ingathering. The meetings were of course held in the lecture room of the new church. At the Quarterly Conference held January, 1877, the pastor reported forty-five taken into the church on probation. Among the probationer's names on the books at this time we find these: Joseph Wells, John Kelfer, George M. Diemer, Ida K.-Finkbiner-Keyser, Willis O. McMichael, John McCann, and S. B. Latshaw.

REVIVAL OF 1878-9.

Revival number seven is sometimes called "The Shields' Revival," since Rev. D. H. Shields was the pastor in charge at this time. He was ably assisted by Rev. Samuel Gracey and the exhorters. This meeting lasted during a long time. *Over one hundred persons* claimed that they had been gathered into the Lord's garner this time. The pastor's historical record, at that time, shows the names of one hundred and twenty-one persons who were admitted on probation. The revival shows how God takes care of his church by sending the increase just when it is so greatly needed. Here are a few of the names: Mrs. Ella-Hunter-Kolb, Mrs. Ida K.-Sheeler-Latshaw, Mrs. Lizzie-Wainwright-Garber, Mrs. Susie R.-Shakespeare-Jones, Levi B. Gearhart, Evans Yeager, John Keeley, and J. Newton Latshaw.

REVIVAL OF 1882-3.

The eighth large revival which we shall record took place during the winter of the above date, under the pastoral charge of Rev. N. D. McComas, assisted by the local ministers, Revs.

S. Gracey, John Flint, and Henry Brook. This note of the meetings is taken from the pastor's report to the Quarterly Conference held on February 9, 1883. "Our revival meeting has continued without interruption. Since last quarter over one hundred persons have been converted, and seventy-nine have joined the church on probation. Forty-nine of these are Sunday-School scholars." The names of Andrew Ortlip, Joseph T. Gracey, R. B. Hunter, Frederick Diemer, W. C. Urner, Bertha A. Taylor, Martha E.-Flint-Dubson, and Lillie C.-Brower-Wagoner, are among the list this time.

REVIVAL OF 1888.

The largest ingathering of souls is perhaps the one now to be chronicled, and we shall call it by its familiar name, "The Ogle Revival," from the fact that the Rev. Thomas G. Ogle, as a special revivalist, conducted the meetings. The Rev. H. B. Cassavant was minister regularly in charge of the pulpit at this time.

The special services commenced in the lecture room of the church in January. Soon this room was too small to seat the surging masses which came nightly through all kinds of weather to the meetings. Then the upper room was thrown open to the services, and sometimes this room was too small.

The revival fire and fervor spread all over the town. The altar at times was not large enough to accommodate the penitents. Room had to be provided at the front seats for those seeking pardon. The meetings were powerful. Those who witnessed the scenes in that upper room, will not soon forget them. Several of the members of the church had written down lists of names of persons for whom special prayers were daily offered. Many of the persons in these lists were affected, came to the altar, gave their hearts to God, and they are now among the best material of the church.

It is hard to set very close figures on the number converted in this four weeks' series of meetings; but it was consid-
erably over one hundred. At the end of the six months' probation period, sixty-nine of them were taken into the church
at one time as full members. September, 1888, was a day in
which one of the most impressive services of the church was
held. On this beautiful Sabbath day the above number of
persons had their names enrolled among those who are in full
connection. Inside the altar stood Rev. J. Bawden, pastor
in charge, some visiting ministers, the local preachers, class
leaders, stewards, and trustees, while outside around the altar,
stood the term-expired probationers in rows two and three
thick, scarcely able to approach near enough to reach through
the line and over the altar railing so as to shake hands with
those who passed in turn around on the inside to extend this
time-honored church custom to them. Now imagine the
whole of these, together with a room-filled audience, many of
whom had tears of joy chasing down over smiling cheeks,
all together singing: "Blest Be the Tie That Binds Our
Hearts in Christian Love," etc. If your mind's eye can recall,
or imagine this scene, you have a picture of something which
cannot be put on canvas, for it is heaven-born, heaven-in-
spired; hence it is a touch of celestial joy! This day's experience will not often be repeated in the life of a single person.

Here is a bunch of the names: Beulah Hunter, A. Grace
Taylor, Cora E. Loomis, J. I. Mowrey, Wayne Forrest, Isaac
Dubson, and Enos F. Grubb.

REVIVAL OF 1891-2.

We place on record as special revival and church up-
building number ten, the refreshing season which visited the
church during the above date. The Rev. Lucian B. Brown

was occupying the pulpit during this time. This revival was not marked by any very sudden outbreak of power, as had some of the previous ingatherings. It was a steady hold-on effort by the church. Earnest pleading with Him, who alone can give the increase, was continued by a faithful church throughout the winter. Prayers freighted with faith and full of unction daily ascended from many hearts. Much closet consecration was practiced, and God greatly blessed the church now as he had so often done before. Many families rejoiced because of dear ones, both children and parents, who were plucked from the clutches of sin.

The revival commenced in December, and as the record shows, probationers were received on trial up to March of the spring following. Eighty new names appeared on the church books this time, the majority of whom were from the Sunday-School. We note these: Misses Mabel R. Hunter, V. Blanche Davis, Ella B. Towers, Mrs. Lidie H.-Keyser-Mowrey, Mrs. Lizzie M.-Keyser-Hunter, Messrs. Granville B. Tyson, and Oliver J. Place.

A Deduction.

We have thus emphasized ten of what seemed to be, at least, among the marked quickenings of the church. There were others which might be brought forward and specialized. During the winter of 1890 and '91 the pulse of the church was made to beat with a great deal of encouragement, Rev. J. Bawden in charge. About forty persons professed to have passed from sin's darkness to the light of salvation during this winter. Again, during Rev. D. Mast Gordon's first winter here, 1894-5, a revival of more than ordinary scope and power visited the church. It lasted for several weeks. About forty names were reached as the result of the Holy Spirit's reaping this time. But perhaps we have described enough.

These revivals were not all alike in power, nor in intensity of fervor. The Holy Spirit seemed to pour out his blessings on the church in various ways. Sometimes God seemed to go through the audience in the whirlwind style, smiting souls on all sides. Then the fire of the Holy Spirit would spread, and all the churches would be quickened. In these cases the meetings might not last so long, perhaps, but they were marked with special power. In other instances "the still small voice" seemed to be the great factor which worked on the hearts of the children of men. But in all these cases God was in the work, and he won the victory. His work went steadily on, and it will continue to move forward as long as the world stands.

In every one of the revivals mentioned, the name of the officiating pastor has been attached. The licensed local talent is also duly credited in the work when it could be done. All glory to them all. We must not, however, conclude this chapter without saying that in all the special efforts put forward by the church for the enlargement of her borders, the pastors were heartily supported by the men and women in the private ranks. In an army battle the commanding general gets the major part of the glory of the victory lavished on him; but it is the missiles of the infantry, the cavalry, the artillery, and the cannon of the navy that do the telling work.

So it is in God's army of the church militant. It will not be disclosed to man in this world how much God has honored the closet service of his devoted followers for their children: children, for parents; neighbors, for neighbors. God has heard; he has spoken to men, and they have responded. Praise God for the revival history of the church militant! May the revival spirit always dominate in the church!

W. C. URNER.

JACOB K. JONES

A. F. TYSON.

M. F. SHEELER

FREDERICK A. DIEMER

IRWIN I. WELLS.

STEWARDS OF SPRING CITY M. E. CHURCH

The Message of the Old Year

By Fanny J. Crosby

Recited by the Author at the
Watch-Night Service of the First Methodist Episcopal Church,
Bridgeport, Conn., December 31, 1905.

List to the clanging bells of time,
　Tolling, tolling a low, sad chime,
A requiem chant o'er the grand Old Year,
　Hark! he is speaking, and bids us hear:

"Friends, I am dying, my hours are few,
　This is the message I leave for you—
'Bought with a price, ye are not your own,
　Live for the Master, and Him alone.

" 'Gather the sheep from the mountains cold,
　Gather them into the Shepherd's fold,
Work for His cause till your work is done,
　Stand by the cross till your crown is won.

" 'Epworth League, there are hosts above
　Watching your labor of zeal and love,
Faithful abide till your days are past,
　Then what a joy will be yours at last.'

"I shall be gone ere the new-born year
　Comes in its beauty the world to cheer:
Once I was young, and my flowers were bright, —
　Think of me kindly.　Good night! Good night!"

CHAPTER VII.

STEWARDS.

At first, while the church was connected with a circuit, there was only one steward from this charge. There were no regular monthly meetings of the Stewards then as now, for the transaction of routine business. In fact, the church in all its forces was not under the organic control which is found everywhere in the work of to-day.

In the early days of our circuit connection it was the duty of the Stewards mainly to see that their share of the finances for supporting the Gospel was raised. The Stewards also attended the Quarterly Conferences and the Quarterly Meetings over the district when the Presiding Elder made his visits for official business. Another duty which fell to these members of the minister's spiritual cabinet, was to meet at a general yearly Steward's Meeting at some convenient place on the Circuit. In this meeting it was ascertained how much financial deficiency was to be made up. This done, the proportionate part of the shortage was alloted to each of the churches on the Circuit, in proportion to the number of members in good standing in the several charges. The Stewards, on their return home from the meetings, reported this state of affairs to the churches. They then proceeded to make up the specified amount.

We notice from some of the tabulated statements on the records of the Circuit, which show the yearly regular contributions, and also the "special collections," that Springville's "special" column occasionally has no amount placed therein.

From this we easily learn that already the amount assigned
to this charge had been paid.

According to the discipline of the church, the preacher
in charge, at the Fourth Quarterly Conference, nominates the
entire Board of Stewards. They are then confirmed and
elected by the Conference. A careful examination of the
Quarterly Conference records shows this list of Stewards,
and their date of service for the Springville-Spring City
Church:—

John Finkbiner, 1855 to 1864; 1868 to 1875.
Edward Brownback, 1864 to 1869.
Samuel Gracey, 1868 to 1875; 1878 to 1881.
Allen Rogers, 1871 to 1877; 1878 to 1890.
Simeon Keim, 1873 to 1878.
John A. Weigel, 1873 to 1876.
Francis M. Hunter, 1875 to 1897.
J. Acker Guss, 1875 to 1876; 1879 to 1888.
John Bisbing, 1875 to 1878.
Jacob R. Weikel, 1875 to 1878.
Morris F. Sheeler, 1876 to 1884; 1887 to 1899.
E. Allen Bickel, 1876 to 1877.
Isaac Shantz, 1877 to 1878.
William H. Fox, 1877 to 1881.
Irwin I. Wells, 1877 to 1878; 1879 to 1880; 1891 to 1899.
John H. Setzler, 1877 to 1878; 1884 to 1888.
Andrew Cummings, 1878 to 1884.
Anderson J. Wright, 1878 to 1879.
John Sheeler, 1878 to 1881.
William S. Essick, 1878 to 1888.
Joseph W. Sheeler, 1880 to 1881; 1882 to 1888.
Jacob K. Jones, 1881 to 1899.

John McCann, 1881 to 1888.
Atmore Loomis, 1884 to 1888.
Josiah M. Nix, 1884 to 1888.
Webster C. Urner, 1884 to 1899.
Robert Forrest, Sr., 1884 to 1887.
John F. Garber, 1884 to 1888.
Herman Ely, 1888 to 1889.
Allen A. Brower, 1888 to 1899.
Joseph Gracey, 1889 to 1893.
John H. Davis, 1889 to 1899.
Joseph I. Mowrey, 1889 to 1899.
Andrew F. Tyson, 1890 to 1899.
W. O. McMichael, 1892 to 1899.
Dr. J. Winfield Good, 1892 to 1899.
Frederick Diemer, 1893 to 1899.
H. Wells Taylor, 1893 to 1897.
Emmanuel Poley, 1896 to 1897.
A. Lincoln Tyson, 1898 to 1899.
J. Walter Sheeler, 1898 to 1899.

RECORDING STEWARDS.

The duty of the Recording Steward is to attend the Quarterly Conferences, when he is able to do so, and to record in a book kept for that special purpose, all the minutes, doings, and reports of the Quarterly Conferences. He is nominated by the pastor of the church, and elected by the Quarterly Conference.

The Recording Stewards thus far are: William M. Staufer, 1855 (?) to 1869; John E. Lewis, 1869 to 1870; Samuel Gracey, 1870 to 1874; J. A. Guss, 1874 to 1876; F. M. Hunter, 1876 to 1878; William S. Essick, 1878 to 1881;

J. A. Guss, 1881 to 1883; William S. Essick, 1883 to 1884; W. C. Urner, 1884 to 1899.

District Stewards.

The duty of this person is to attend the Annual District Stewards' Meeting in Philadelphia, when called by the Presiding Elder. He there has a voice in this meeting which provides for the comfort of the Presiding Elder and the Bishop. The proportionate amount of money to be raised by every church for the Elder and the Bishop is also fixed at this meeting.

Some of the District Stewards thus far are: William M. Staufer, William L. Bingaman, Edward Brownback, John Finkbiner, John Sheeler, J. A. Guss, William S. Essick, F. M. Hunter, J. K. Jones, and M. F. Sheeler.

Trustees.

In the year 1855 five persons were appointed by the Quarterly Conference of Pottstown Circuit as Trustees, and they were especially instructed to purchase the Union Meeting House at Springville, so as "to establish a regular preaching station" in that thriving little village. Their names are cited in the deed which passed the title from Mr. James Rogers, Sr., and wife, to the possession of the Methodists. Of these five, four soon moved away, thus leaving only one, Mr. John Finkbiner, to assume the obligations of looking after the financial interests of the church; and this he did nobly. Often he put his hand into his own pocket and paid the bills which were assumed by the church. *For thirteen years* this faithful gentleman constituted *the entire Trustee Board* of the Springville Methodist Episcopal Church; for there is no record or knowledge, so far as we have been able to learn, of the appoint-

ment of any additional Trustees until the session of the
Fourth Quarterly Conference, which was held at Coventryville on January 26, 1868. At this Conference, Presiding
Elder J. Castle in the chair, Trustees were appointed all over
the Circuit to serve their charges. The first seven on the list
appended herewith were appointed for Springville Church.

CHARTER.

The Trustees are now somewhat guided by a Charter.
But up to the year 1872, they were appointed by the Quarterly Conference, first being nominated by the preacher in
charge. In the above named year, the year in which the old
church building was removed and the new one commenced,
application was made to the courts of Chester County, Pa.,
for a Charter of Incorporation. This was granted. It bears
the name of S. G. Williams as Prothonotary, and it is dated
October 31, 1872.

The Trustee Board, which came into official capacity
with the Charter, was: President, Samuel Gracey; Secretary,
John E. Lewis; Treasurer, Jacob Keiter; Allen Rogers, John
Finkbiner, Simeon Keim, William Priest, F. R. Guss, and
John B. Gracey. A code of by-laws, divided into fifteen well-
worded sections, now controls the actions of the Board. By
the provision of these by-laws three Trustees are elected, by
ballot, on the first Thursday of December of every year, and
they serve for three years. The electors required for choos-
ing trustees are all the members of the church who are over
twenty-one years of age, and in good standing in the church.
It will thus be seen that this important board of management,
whose duty it is to care for the temporal affairs of the church,
is a perpetual board. One-third of its members are elected
every year. Here is the list of Trustees since 1855, with
their terms of service:—

John Finkbiner, 1855 to 1899.

Edward Brownback, 1868 to 1869.

Samuel Gracey, 1868 to 1873.

Jacob Keiter, 1868 to 1878.

Allen Rogers, 1868 to 1880.

John E. Lewis, 1868 to 1874.

William Priest, 1868 to 1874.

James Swindells, 1873 to 1876.

Simeon Keim, 1873 to 1878.

Francis M. Hunter, 1874 to 1878.

Jacob R. Weikel, 1874 to 1878; 1879 to 1899.

Emmanuel S. Crater, 1874 to 1876.

John A. Weikel, 1874 to 1878.

Isaac Shantz, 1876 to 1877; 1891 to 1896.

E. Allen Bickel, 1876 to 1899.

William H. Fox, 1877 to 1880.

Jonathan Seazholtz, 1878 to 1879.

Irwin I. Wells, 1878 to 1882; 1889 to 1890.

Morris F. Sheeler, 1878 to 1887.

Andrew Cummings, 1878 to 1888.

John B. Gracey, 1878 to 1891.

John A. Keiter, 1879 to 1899.

Samuel B. Latshaw, 1880 to 1887.

Jesse G. Yeager, 1882 to 1899.

Nehemiah Sheeder, 1887 to 1891.

Joseph H. Benjamin, 1889 to 1896.

Hiram Bickhart, 1890 to 1893.

Enos F. Grubb, 1892 to 1899.

John F. Garber, 1893 to 1896.

Anthony Vanhook, 1896 to 1899.

Thomas G. Wynn, 1896 to 1899.

Uriah Garber, 1896 to 1899.

LOCAL PREACHERS.

"Preach the Word." 2 Timothy 4:2.

The Local Preacher has always been, and he still is, a wonderfully valuable aid to the pastor in charge and to his church as well. In starting out on work he occasionally was required to deliver one or more of his efforts in the presence of his pastor. If his theology, energy, talents, and delivery were satisfactory to the pastor, a license was given to our young man at once, and he "was harnessed" up ready for the pulpit. Sometimes he had to preach a "trial sermon" in the presence of the Presiding Elder also.

The first local preacher at this charge was Rev. Samuel Graccy, 1859. The records show that these followed him:—

J. D. Flansburg, 1867.
James Swindells, 1870.
Frederick R. Guss, 1872.
Henry Brook, 1872.
Caleb L. Hughes, 1873.
John Flint, 1879.
Andrew M. Ortlip, 1886.
Benjamin La Pish, 1888.
Edwin A. Bawden, 1889.
Ernest Bawden, 1891.
Reuben B. Hunter, 1898.

EXHORTERS.

"He (Barnabas) was glad, and exhorted them all, that with purpose of heart they would cleave unto the Lord." Acts 11:23.

One of the wisely adjusted affairs in the economy of the Methodist Episcopal Church is, that she tries to train her

children to express themselves while standing on their feet.
The exhorter begins to talk in the class room, afterward,
perhaps, in the prayer meeting or in the revival service. Yes;
all the Great Lights of the Methodist Episcopal Church have
gone through this spiritual training school. They have ac-
quired the art of talking, by talking. The line of their promotion up the church ladder is exhorter, local preacher, itin-
erant, Presiding Elder, and finally Bishop. Here is the list
of those who, in some way, have been connected with the
church here:—

David Wells, 1855.
Samuel Gracey, 1858.
Frederick R. Guss, 1870.
Joseph Gearhart, 1872.
Simeon Keim, 1875.
John Flint, 1879.
Morris F. Sheeler, 1880.
William S. Essick, 1880.
Jesse G. Yeager, 1884.
Jacob K. Jones, 1884.
Francis M. Hunter, 1884.
Benjamin La Pish, 1886.
John F. Garber, 1888.
Joseph A. Coulston, 1891.
Reuben B. Hunter, 1891.

CHAPTER VIII.

THE MINISTERS.

These devout men on whom the hand of God and that of the Church, as well, has been laid, deserve a share of our attention at this point in our narrative. An inquiry into the personnel of these ecclesiastical worthies who preached on the old Pottstown Circuit reveals the fact that fidelity to the cause which they espoused was always manifested. As the charges were separated from one another, much inconvenience was experienced in going from place to place to meet the preaching engagements. Ministers often risked their health. They traveled through storm and sunshine. All kinds of weather found them in the saddle or carriage going to serve their people. Often after a long ride against a cold, wintry blast, they were compelled to preach in an atmosphere which was very hard on the human system. They often stood in the pulpit and delivered their sacred message with wet clothes on their backs, as well as with wet feet.

The sermons of those *antebellum* days were not always so full of school lore as the sermons of to-day are; but they were full of the Word of God, and that gave power to them. Lack of time prevented, to a good degree, pulpit preparation. Hence many of the pulpit efforts which passed for preaching at that time, would be called first-class exhortations in the present day. But it served the purpose of the Master. It is now proposed to develop this subject further under the Captions of *Entertainment, Support,* and *The Ministers Themselves.*

I. ENTERTAINING THE MINISTERS.

When this charge was a part of the Circuit, a committee was always appointed at one of the Quarterly Conferences, and the duty of said committee was to rent a suitable house at some convenient place in which the Senior Preacher and his family might reside. This residence was generally at Coventryville, or at Pottstown. The rent of the parsonage was apportioned among the several charges, according to the number of members at each charge. As a rule it was collected by special contributions, taken at the end of the Conference year. The furnishing of the parsonage was done in the same way. This report is on the Quarterly Conference minutes of August 8, 1863: "Bro. D. W. Gordon, Committee on raising funds for parsonage carpet, reports having collected $23.95 for the same."

The Junior Preacher had a place provided for him, generally with the family of a farmer; but sometimes the single man made his home elsewhere. Here he made, at least, his headquarters, and then went about among the charges and worked as his Senior brother directed him. His business was to receive and to execute orders. At times he had only one room in which to domicile. This room served him for his parlor, his library, study, and sleeping-room as well. Generally the Junior was fortunate enough to obtain two rooms for his apartments. Then he was more comfortably equipped.

The Junior, as well as the Senior, generally had a horse and carriage. The horse either belonged to the Church, or it was loaned to the minister by some one of the church members.

This state of affairs continued until the year 1872, when Rev. J. H. Wood was sent to take charge of the church at Springville and Bethel Circuit. The men who had preached at Spring City prior to this date had all been single men, with the exception of the Seniors. Rev. Richard Turner had been married just before going to Conference in the spring of 1872, and Rev. Mr. Wood was married just after he had come from Conference in the same year. These were the first ministers who were married while in charge of the church at Springville.

We have drifted a little aside from our story. Let us go back and look after some of our single preachers. Rev. J. P. Miller was the first minister who was provided with home accommodations in the borough by the church. This was in the year 1868. Two rooms were fitted out for him with Mr. Josiah Schick, now No. 34 South Main Street. In 1869 he domiciled with Mr. E. A. Bickel at No. 167 Chestnut Street. Rev. Richard Turner came in 1870. During his first year he made his home at Mr. John Betz's on the Schuylkill Road, second year at Mr. E. A. Bickel's and at Mr. F. R. Guss's on West Bridge Street.

When Rev. Mr. Wood changed his relation in life, he furnished his house partly at his own expense with what he and his good wife needed. They commenced housekeeping on West Bridge Street in the house with Mr. F. R. Guss. Soon one end of Mr. Philip Simon's house, No. 140 New Street, was rented as the *First Parsonage* of the Spring City M. E. Church. Here Mr. and Mrs. Wood lived during their two years' sojourn with our people. Rev. Eli Pickersgill lived first on Main Street, then at No. 137 Chestnut Street. In Rev. D. H. Shields's time the parsonage was, first year at the corner of New and Church Streets, and, second year, at No.

129 New Street, where the parsonage remained until the
year of 1884 when the minister, Rev. N. D. McComas, moved
into the present parsonage on Hall Street.

NEW PARSONAGE.

At the Quarterly Conference held February 9, 1883,
Messrs. M. F. Sheeler, J. G. Yeager. S. B. Latshaw, John
Finkbiner, and Atmore Loomis were appointed as a Parsonage Building Committee to see that a suitable building be
erected on the south end of the church lot. This building
was to be finished so as to be a suitable place for the family
of the minister. They immediately set to work with the duties
before them, and by March, 1884, the present parsonage was
the result of their labors. As already shown, Rev. N. D.
McComas was the preacher in charge at that time, and he
occupied the new parsonage one year.

When the building committee made their final report to
the Conference, it was shown that the entire cost of the building was *Two Thousand Eight Hundred* and *Eighteen Dollars
and two cents*. This does not include the value of the lot, as
the church already owned that. The greater part of the above
expenditures had already been met by subscriptions.

II. SUPPORT OF THE MINISTERS.

In the years before the Rebellion. ministers in the country charges at least. often received a very meager financial
income for their labors. But this was partly overcome by
the farmers who would always remember their pastor in some
substantial manner. This would be done by a well-filled
basket of vegetables or fruits. which was often left at the
parsonage. At butchering time a lot of good things was sure

SPRING CITY M. E. PARSONAGE

to find its way to the parson's cellar from the generous hands of the church members. A few bushels of potatoes and apples came there in the same way. So while the minister of the Gospel might not have had a very large bank account standing to his credit, his cellar was filled often with the good things which help to make up a good round meal. This was particularly the case on the old Pottstown Circuit. It was also, to some extent, the custom after the ministers began to reside at Spring City.

We are not able to ascertain very closely the amount of money paid to the pastors from this charge, because the collections were all gathered into one general fund while on the Circuit, then paid to the ministers. As already stated, the Junior ministers at first received *One Hundred Dollars* a year for their services. At the outbreak of the Rebellion, 1862, the Junior's salary was made Two Hundred Dollars. In the year 1865, when the Springville church had been regularly served for ten years, the Quarterly Conference minutes show that the Preacher in charge received Six Hundred and Fifty Dollars for his services; One Hundred Dollars of this was for traveling expenses. The Junior Preacher this year received for his efforts Two Hundred Dollars. Thus, just at the close of the Rebellion, when commodities of all kinds were very high in price, the Revs. S. G. Hare and T. O. Tompkins, the ministers then in charge, must have been compelled to practice severe economy in order to meet their expenses. Rev. Tompkins was expected to pay his boarding at this time.

A tabulated report for the above year is here given, which shows the apportionment of the different charges for the support of the gospel, and for the rent of the parsonage which was then at Pottstown:—

	Apportionment.	Rent.
Coventry	$174 90	$9 54
Bethel	174 90	9 54
Pottstown	168 30	9 18
Nantmeal	158 40	8 64
Ebenezer	132 00	7 20
Springville	112 20	6 12
Total	$920 70	$50 22

This year the Presiding Elder received from the Circuit Seventy Dollars; and Forty Dollars were paid for parsonage rent.

Ten years later, and the second year after the Spring City M. E. Church attempted to stand on her own feet and become a separate charge, Eight Hundred Dollars were raised and paid to the pastor: One Hundred and Twenty Dollars for rent, Fifty-four Dollars for the Elder and the Bishop, besides the expenses of the Trustees. In all, during this year, 1875, *Twelve Hundred Dollars* were required to defray the current expenses of the church. In 1885, after the lapse of another decade, the running expenses of the church were about the same as in 1875. In 1885 the pastor's salary was advanced to One Thousand Dollars, and since 1892 Twelve Hundred Dollars a year have been paid to the shepherd of the flock.

In the Philadelphia Conference there are four churches which now pay their pastor Three Thousand Dollars a year; three which pay Two Thousand Five Hundred Dollars; eleven which pay Two Thousand Dollars, and One Hundred and Seventeen which pay One Thousand Dollars and upwards.

III. WHAT THE MINISTERS THEMSELVES SAY.

It is the province of the historian to chronicle events, not as he thinks they should be, but as they really have

A GROUP OF CIRCUIT PREACHERS

transpired. He may desire to record matters in a much different way from that in which he finds them. He dares not do it. Much care must be exercised by him, as he uses his brush, in coloring facts. This has constantly been the aim in sketching the events recorded in this book.

We have already collected from the records and from the memory of those whose mental storehouse of facts seemed to be trustworthy, the material given heretofore. An effort will now be made to let some of the ministers themselves speak of the work as they found it, when they came upon the theatre of labor and love over the Circuit. Springville formerly was only a part and parcel of a great ecclesiastical plan to spread the Gospel, and win souls for the heavenly mansions, mentioned in the fourteenth chapter of St. John's Gospel. It will thus easily be seen that it is no easy task for an historical writer to draw the severing knife among a well-planned system of closely united preaching stations and separate them without, at least, doing some of the others a little injustice. In the day of chivalrous Methodism on the old Pottstown Circuit, what was Springville's history was, to a great extent, the history of eight or more other charges. They were all bound together as one band of workers in Christian fellowship, and the manipulation of the working forces was under the guidance of the Senior preachers, who received their authority and instructions as well, from the Bishop.

In order to give to our readers an idea of how the work was done somewhat in detail, a circular letter containing some questions was sent out to several of the ministers, asking them to reply to the inquiries as best they could. The ministers interrogated were selected so as to cover the church's history since the year 1854. As nearly all of them are unknown to the writer, they have been chosen to speak for no special purpose; but simply to tell how they saw the work, and to speak "without fear or favor." Here are the questions and the replies. We shall introduce the speakers *by number*, and give the date when they were on the Circuit, or at Spring City alone.

By referring to the proper date in the list of ministers on page 159, the reader can learn the name of the person whose quotations are hereby produced.

Question 1.—*"Where did you make your home while here? And what were your surroundings?"*

Minister *Number One*, 1854, is now presented to you. He speaks as follows: "I was a single man, and Junior preacher. The Rev. Abram Freed was my superintendent, and he was the responsible man. The First Quarterly Conference of that year voted that I should have a boarding place. Brothers Frees and Essick, of Coventryville, together with myself, were appointed to secure one. We found a home with Mr. Louis Stubblebine at Coventryville. I had one room, which answered as study and bed room. It was carpeted and conveniently furnished. I had also a good stable for my horse, and a carriage house for my carriage and harness."

Clergyman *Number Two*, whose sainted locks are now assuming the hue of the robes in heaven, steps forward and occupies the interrogatory chair. He unsheathes his spectacles, carefully removes the dusty film from the same, looks back through the vista of Forty-three winters, focuses his intellectual lenses on the scenes of his first ministry, and this is what he says about it:—

"I was appointed on the Pottstown Circuit by Bishop Beverly Waugh. I was Junior preacher, with Rev. Abram Freed as preacher in charge. This was in March, 1855, and it was my first year in the Conference on trial. I had very little to do but to preach three times every Sabbath, and to obey the orders of my superiors in succession, from the Bishop down.

"The Junior preacher was expected to live among the people. This I did to some extent. The First Quarterly Conference granted me a home. I got one with a Mrs. McFarland, a Baptist lady in Coventryville. I kept some books and clothes there, but I had to be out on the Circuit most of the time. I kept a horse, but I had to buy his feed. So, altogether for the preacher's boarding and horse feed, it only cost the Circuit about *Twenty-eight Dollars* for the year, and *Seventy-six Dollars* for salary. One Hundred Dollars was the allowance for the Junior preacher's salary; but Brother Freed had five children and had to keep a horse and carriage, and as he was short of receiving his allotted Five Hundred Dollars for salary, they took Twenty-four Dollars off me, since I was not married. I preached at Springville once a month in the evening. My home was with Brother David Wells several times, on a farm between Springville and Bethel (where Mr. Seneca Mowrey now lives). Another very nice stopping place was at Mr. Edward Brownback's (where Mr. Isaac Funk now lives). It was a nice home in the summer, but awfully cold in the winter. In the village (Springville) I had more places at which to stop over night than I could fill. I well remember one brother there whose name was John Finkbiner, who still lives to praise God and do good. He had been converted before I knew him. He was then full of fire and the Holy Ghost, as I believe he remains to-day. But he is *nearer Home than ever he was before.*"

Pastor *Number Three.* Seven years have now elapsed since Junior *Number Two* traveled over the Coventries and the Nantmeals. We now place before us *Number Three*. He looks back through Thirty-six summers of his life, reviews the events of 1862 as he met them, and this is how he tells the story:—

"I was appointed by Bishop Scott in March, 1862, as Junior preacher on the Pottstown Circuit. Rev. Valentine Gray, of precious memory, was the preacher in charge. The Circuit then contained seven churches: Pottstown, Coventry, Ebenezer, Nantmeal, Bethel, St. John's, and Springville.

"I was unmarried, and I made my home at Coventry with Rev. John Watson. It was expected that I would spend most of my time among the families of the Circuit. My salary, Two Hundred Dollars, was intended to be adequate for all my necessary expenses, including board for myself and horse. I was not as well provided for as I had been at former charges, where I never had to use my salary to pay boarding and lodging. I did not complain, because even this was more than other Junior preachers had been receiving. When I was at Springville I generally made my home at Brother Edward Brownback's, or Brother William Priest's. They had accommodations for my horse."

Minister *Number Four* now occupies the chair just made vacant by Number Three. A decade has elapsed between their labors. This earth of ours on which there is so much of struggle for supremacy, power, and preference, has made ten of its annual trips around the sun since Junior *Number Three's* time. Changes occurred in every trip. Ten times the picturesque hills and charming vales of the Pottstown Circuit have been carpeted with the snows of winter. As often have the productive meadows and the fertile hillsides brought forth the sweet-scented flowers of spring, the golden harvests of summer, and the ripe fruits of autumn. Six of the Senior ministers have come upon the scene, and spent their efforts at giving direction to the work of soul-saving. They have nobly done their work, and gone to other fields of labor. These Seniors had, during this time, five of the Junior preachers, who sustained them in the work. Many of the servants of the Lord over the District have answered the death-call and have gone home to join the Church triumphant. Others have come forward to take the places just vacated. The Lord's work is moving forward. The six charges served by Number Three and his co-laborer in the Master's Vineyard have, by Conference division and adjustment, been reduced to two. The work has grown in importance, both spiritually and temporally. We shall be glad to listen to this, now, Doctor of Divinity tell his story of labor, triumph, and love.

"I was appointed to Springville, or Spring City, and Bethel charge in March, 1872. I went there a married man. For three months we lived with the family of one of our local preachers, Mr. F. R. Guss, on Bridge Street. We had the privilege of their entire house and barn. We were treated kindly. A part of the time we boarded with the family, and the remainder of the time we kept our own table. We then took a vacation for the summer. A part of this time I boarded with Mr. Gideon Weikel on Main Street. In the early fall we went to housekeeping in a new three-story house which we rented of Mr. Philip Simon, on New Street. We had a very pleasant house.

"The church paid half of the rent, and we paid the remainder. We did the same with the house furnishing. The church owned the horse, and the pastor was the possessor of the harness and the carriage. We went halves in this way, as the charge had previously been a single man's appointment; yet the church did what they could to make us comfortable, and we supplied deficiencies."

Clergyman *Number Five*, 1879, you surely will all greet with kindness, as his sympathetic face is known to most of the readers of this little volume. His earnest, pathetic, and soul-moving sermons still reverberate in the hearts of many people in Spring City to-day, after a lapse of twenty years. Here is the way he speaks to you:—

"I was a single man when appointed, but married two weeks later and lived on New Street. The church was generous enough to ask me to furnish the parlor, and this I did."

Question 2.—"*What do you remember about the revival work?*"

To this question minister *Number One* says: "I was only on the Circuit three months. I left on the first of July. There was no revival work during my stay."

Let us call *Number Two* again. Hear him: "We held five extra meetings at five different churches that fall and winter, commencing in October and continuing until Conference. Then the other five churches were served the next winter. Brother Freed considered that Springville was a new and special charge, needing his personal oversight. So he gave me very little to do there outside of my regular appointments. I was there during Protracted Meeting about eight evenings. The meetings were excellent; many were saved. The number I never learned as they were all lumped in with the report of the Circuit. But I remember that there were some substantial converts. We had fifty conversions reported on the Conference minutes, as the number for the whole Circuit, that year."

How *Number Three* answers this question: "I commenced a Protracted Meeting, as it was called in those days, at Springville, on Wednesday evening, November 19th, and preached from James 5:20. Thursday and Friday evenings were rainy, and we had no meeting. On Sunday I preached at 3 P.M. and administered the sacrament of the Lord's Supper. In the evening I preached again. The meeting continued for about three weeks. The preaching all fell to my lot but a couple of evenings when Brother Valentine Gray preached. I also preached a Thanksgiving Day sermon on Thursday, November 27, at 10 A.M., from Psalms 116:12-14. A few souls professed conversion at our meetings. On December 5th a large snow storm came on and interrupted the meetings. On Sunday morning following I preached from Jer. 13: 16, to a crowded house. Many people came in from the surroundings in sleighs, strangers who had not been at the meetings before.

"On the Sunday following I had to preach at Pottstown, morning and night. We had several Protracted Meetings to hold, and as winter was on us, the meeting at Springville was discontinued. I regretted closing the meeting without a great revival. At times there were indications of it, but it seemed so hard to persuade people under conviction to come to the altar. I had a great desire to see prosperity at Springville. I conceived a promising future for Methodism there. I think if we had continued the meetings, the Lord's blessing on faithful labor would have been crowned with success. I was anxious to see the church prosper, for as the town was growing at that time, I wanted the church to be like a city on a hill, shedding her light on all around."

Number Four.—"We had many conversions, many of whom remain as good members in Spring City, and also in the church which was afterward built at Royersford. Some have gone on before, and we expect to greet them there."

Number Five.—"I followed Rev. David H. Shields under whose ministry there had been a marked revival. I found about *One Hundred and Twenty-five* probationers to be helped, most of whom were received in full connection. I glean from my private record these statistics:—

"'Received on probation during my term of three years, 70; received by certificate, 33; baptized, 91; married, 23 couples; attended 54 funerals; money collected from all sources, $10,500.'"

Note—While the tying of nuptial knots is mostly an accident to the Methodist minister, yet the number above is the largest one on the records of the church at this place. Rev. D. Mast Gordon joined the second largest number of happy couples, namely: thirteen.

Question 3.—"*How did the work here compare with your work at other charges?*"

Number One.—"There were eight regular appointments, and I preached on Saturday evenings at Douglasville School House, making nine. It was the longest Circuit I ever had. But as I was there during the pleasantest part of the year, I cannot say that the work was especially hard."

Number Two speaks again. He gives the programme for preaching. Here it is: "We had ten appointments for Sabbath, and Douglasville School House extra for Saturday evenings. I preached at Birdsboro at 10.30 A.M., and held Sunday class meetings after preaching; High's School House at 3.30 P.M.; Pottstown at 8 P.M. On the next Sunday: Pottstown at 10.30 A.M., Temple at 3 P.M., and Pottstown at night. On the Sunday following I had Nantmeal in the morning and evening, and Ebenezer at 3 P.M. The fourth Sunday I preached at Coventryville in the morning, Bethel in the afternoon, and Springville at night.

"I don't wish to boast, but I shall give you an idea of the work of a young preacher of that day on a large Circuit. I rode on horseback from Nantmeal to Birdsboro on Saturday, preached there on Sunday morning, then through very deep snow to High's School House, four miles. After preaching there in the afternoon, again rode to Pottstown, five miles, often just arriving there in time to ascend the pulpit in the evening for preaching, then prayer meeting. After services I cleaned and fed my horse and got to bed at eleven or twelve o'clock. Next day I mounted my horse again and rode through the snow, nine miles, to Nantmeal and continued the revival meetings for the week. Brother Freed was at the same time holding meetings somewhere else. It was not always so severe, but very often it was. The mud in the spring time was nearly as bad as the snows of winter."

Number Three's version of it: "Pottstown Circuit was a laborious charge. The roads were rough and hilly, and a minister was much exposed to inclement weather in going his rounds of duty. It was fatiguing to both man and horse, more so than charges which I had previously served. Then again, the snows were a great hindrance to us. I well remember the snow storm of December 5th, and the severely cold weather which followed. I could not use my carriage, so I went on horseback. I rode from Coventry to Ebenezer while the snow was drifting so badly that my horse could scarcely get through it. When I arrived there only one person had come to church. I then returned to Coventry, and after an early supper I rode to Springville through the drifts as best I could."

Number Four.—"One great event of my pastorate at Spring City was the erection of the new church. I shall leave to others a description of the old building, but will just say in passing that I came near breaking my neck by falling through the old steps on my way to preach the first Sabbath evening. I went into the pulpit and said, among other things, 'Brethern, the Lord must have a new house here,' and they responded, *Amen!* The new church enterprise was soon launched. Brother John Finkbiner subscribed and paid the first Thousand Dollars."

Number Five.—"The work was rather more of fatigue than of mental anxiety as compared with former charges. This was owing largely to two causes. And the first was the pastoral care of such a large number of probationers: and the second was the careful oversight required in so much church building.

"But I enjoyed the work, and have always done so in all the years of my ministry. I enjoyed the work there particularly, because there was an earnest activity among most of the brethren. This suited me exactly. I like to see things go, and they went at that charge, and I believe they do so yet."

Question 4.—"*Compare the church's ability here to meet her financial obligations; also, her treatment of the ministers with that of other churches which you have served.*"

Number One.—"I was kindly received and well treated at all the appointments except Pottstown. The society there was small and distant and very cold."

Number Two.—"In my time the Circuit was very poor; it had ten churches, but in all, only 364 members. They raised for the Missionary Collection, $140; Bible Collection, $20; Education, $10; Sunday-School Union, $23; Conference Collections, $30; Rev. Freed's house rent was $75. These amounts, added to the preachers' salaries, made the grand total of $913 for the year *on the whole Circuit.*

"The membership at Springville was not large nor strong, yet I remember Brother Freed holding them up as an example of liberality to older and larger charges on the Circuit. They were certainly the most liberal and spiritual people for their number on the whole Circuit. They were a *laborious, earnest, self-denying,* and *generous* people."

Number Three.—"I think they fully met all their financial obligations. My salary, I know, was promptly paid by the Circuit, and I am quite sure Springville paid her share. The collections on sacramental occasions and other collections that I took were comparatively the best on the Circuit.

"I was quite happy in my relation to the Springville church. I was treated with respect, and by the church and community I was honored. There was such a sincerity and a good degree of spirituality in our congregations. Our class meetings there were precious seasons, inspiring and encouraging me in my arduous and responsible work."

Number Four.—"At the close of my two years' pastorate the two charges were made separate stations, each with its own regular pastor. During my sojourn with the people of Spring City ties of friendship and love were formed which have already stood the test of years; and I firmly believe they will continue throughout eternity."

Number Five.—"The church met its financial obligations fairly well, all things considered, as will be indicated in my next answer. Sometimes I have thought that others who did and gave far less, were much more fully appreciated."

Question 5.—"*Give any additional facts, social or otherwise, which may be of interest.*"

Number One.—"I enjoyed my work and my relations with the people. I have some very pleasant memories of my three months' stay on that Circuit. Mr. and Mrs. Lacy of Birdsboro, Mr. Binder of Ebenezer, Father Christman, Brothers Frees and Bingaman of Coventryville, are some of the names of people who were very considerate. The only name which I can now call up from your Spring City, or Royersford, is Brother John Finkbiner.

"I think I preached in a school-house that stood on the same street on which your splendid church now stands."

Note—He means the Union Meeting House, the basement of which at that time was used for public school purposes.

Number Two.—"I think the church had been built as a Union Church, and the Methodists had got control of it either that year or the year before I came. Brother Freed, I remember, gave me a book when I went on the Circuit, to collect money with which to help clear the church debt. I did what I could, but I do not know how much I collected. I soon returned the book and the money to Brother Freed.

"My work I enjoyed very much. The only exception I had to it was that I did not have time enough to prepare my sermons. My Conference studies were also constantly on my mind."

Number Three.—"While the Confederate army were trying to invade Pennsylvania, and just two days before the Battle of Antietam, September 15th, a war meeting was held in Mechanics' Hall in the evening. Captain Dobson of Phœnixville, being sick, had returned home from the seat of war. He was to address this meeting. The captain was present; but he was so weak he could not stand to talk. He attempted to address the meeting sitting in his chair, but the carnage he had seen on the field of battle came so vividly before his mind that his feelings in his weak, nervous state overcame him, and he could not continue his address.

"Rev. Valentine Gray and myself, who were also present, were then called upon to speak. Rev. Mr. Gray spoke; then I followed. I did not want to speak at all, but as I had just come from a six years' preaching experience south of Mason and Dixon's line, on the eastern shore of Maryland, they insisted on my coming to the platform and giving them my impressions of the secession movement as I had become acquainted with it, while with those people. This I did as best I could. The meeting was enthusiastic and full of patriotic sentiment. A large number gave their names as volunteers to protect the border.

"Many of the scenes of those days come up vividly before my mind. Well do I remember the visitations I made to the home of Brother James Gracey, father of our worthy local preacher, Rev. Samuel Gracey. We always had profitable conversations on religious subjects. He was a good man, and very Methodistic. His religion was very experimental. He could say 'For I know whom I have believed, and am persuaded that he is able to keep that which I have committed unto him against that day.' I always was encouraged in the Master's work after a visit to that family. Brother Gracey consecrated his family to God, and it is quite natural that a son should become a useful local preacher.

"Brother John Finkbiner I also remember. He had an open hand and a warm heart. He was in sympathy with every need of the church. A willing worker was he, ready to bear a part of every burden, and always at the front of every forward movement. Surely he was a true servant of the Lord.

"Another brother whose impression is indelibly fixed on my mind was Edward Brownback. Well did he know what experimental religion is. His light shone brightly in every department of worship. His words in class meetings, his prayers, and his singing, were accompanied with a spirit that permeated all hearts and brought them into the unity of peace, love, and joy. I enjoyed hearing him sing 'A HUNDRED YEARS TO COME.' He sang it with a pathos which so moved my feelings that I enjoyed the sentiment in an unusual manner. It seems but yesterday that I heard him sing that beautiful hymn, yet more than one-third of a hundred years have gone since that time. Thirty-six years have fled away into the past; he is with the redeemed, singing the song of 'Moses and the Lamb.' We are here in the Church Militant, having our conflicts and triumphs; our trials and temptations; our sorrows and rejoicings. Our experience is a mingling of fear and hope, weakness and strength, darkness and light. This is not heaven, it is the battlefield, a warfare.

> The saints, in all this glorious war,
>   Shall conquer, though they die;
> They see the triumph from afar,
>   By faith they bring it nigh.

"The church was on a hill side. We worshiped on the second floor, and had to go up many steps into the room.

EDWARD BROWNBACK

A FORMER STEWARD AT SPRING CITY M. E. CHURCH

This used to suggest to me the thought of climbing up Zion's hill.

"There was a small membership. Their spiritual state was very good. The Sunday-School was prosperous. The congregations were small, but they continued to increase.

"They had a choir which discoursed music better than usual for a small society. I think their leader was a teacher of vocal music, and the young people in the choir belonged to his class. I do not remember the name of the choir leader. But well do I remember they used to sing the tune AMERICA, with the parts."

Note.—The chorister referred to above was Mr. George K. Hoffman.

Number Five.—"When I was appointed to Spring City, the basement of our church was the only place of religious worship in the town. Brother Neff's people (Lutheran) met in an old school-house, subsequently changed into a janitor's home. During my first year the main audience room was finished and dedicated at a cost of about Two Thousand Four Hundred Dollars. This was one of the best pieces of financiering I have known.

"During my third year the first church at Royersford was built, paid for, and dedicated. Bishop Simpson performed the rites of dedication.

"I may further add as a matter of possible interest, that on August 27, 1879, our oldest daughter, Mary E., was born. She is now a young lady in her nineteenth year."

Answers from other divines might easily have been added, but these are sufficient to give the reader an idea of how the work appeared, as seen by the broadcloth faternity. Three of the men whose replies are appended to the queries were Junior Preachers, and two of them had the entire charge of the church's affairs. As will be noticed, all alike had the burden of souls and the advancement of the Master's kingdom at heart.

This article would, no doubt, have been enriched with other experiences and impressions, if some of the Senior Preachers could have sat before us in their easy chairs and told how they met and surmounted the difficulties of manipulating a large Circuit. But those sainted men of God have either all left the Conference, or they have gone to their reward in Glory. We have not been able to find any of them.

Reference has been made above by some of the ministers to the names of church members over the Circuit, who were wont to be very considerate in caring for the physical necessities of their pastors. There were also many other members of the church who always held out a liberal hand at entertaining the parson. A few of them are here appended.

At Ebenezer, Mr. Jonathan Mauger and his good helpmate took care of the minister when he came that way. Messrs. Joseph Cloud, Daniel Walley, and Daniel Simmers vied with one another at Nantmeal in caring for their pastor. They all were well pleased to have the parson sit at table with them and partake of a farmer's rations.

Foremost among those who had the preacher stop with them at Coventry was Mr. Jacob Sheeler, a life-long Methodist. When the parson drove up to Mr. Sheeler's hitching-post, willing hands soon unhitched the horse, put him away to a good mess of oats and an arm full of hay. And they did it all without expecting to have the minister drop a fippenny-bit in their hands when he drove away. Yes: an extra plate and chair were soon at Mr. Sheeler's table if Mr. Dominie happened around about meal time. Mr. William Essick was another farmer at Coventry who had a good deal of experience in entertaining the preacher. At Bethel, when the preachers came around, they often tied up at Mr. Jacob Keiter's or at Mr. Joseph Bachman's. Messrs. John Garber and William M. Staufer shared their hospitalities with the spiritual advisers also.

CHAPTER IX.

AUXILIARIES.

I. THE LADIES' AID SOCIETY.

The history of the Methodist Episcopal Church in Spring City would not be complete without a sketch of the doings of the Ladies' Aid Society. Indeed this band of loyal Christian women has done a good work in their sphere, and they have done it well.

On Thursday afternoon, September 4, 1872, just four days before the corner-stone of the new church was laid, a number of ladies met at the home of Mrs. Annie M. Gracey, No. 43 Church Street, drew up and signed the constitution and by-laws, and organized a working band under the name of "The Ladies' Aid Society of Spring City M. E. Church." Their constitution shows that the object of the society "is to promote the interests of the Spring City M. E. Church in such manner as shall be determined by vote of the society."

The first officers were: President, Miss Maggie Swindells; Vice-president, Mrs. Lizzie Bailey; Secretary, Mrs. Kate C. Guss, and Treasurer, Mrs. Annie M. Gracey, who has held this office ever since. The society members pay a monthly dues of Ten Cents each, meet once a month in regular session, and occasionally hold special sessions. One of the aims of the society is to look after the temporal affairs of the parsonage. They see that things are all in good comfortable trim at the home of the pastor. They also meet every incoming pastor and his family at the parsonage, and see that they have a good royal welcome.

In their earlier history festivals were held under their direction. As an example, we mention a fair and ice cream festival which was held under the direction of a committee appointed by the Ladies' Aid. This festival was held for three consecutive evenings in the unfinished upper room of the church in June, 1873. So careful were they of the manner of conducting the affair that no chancing, or questionable methods of any kind whatever were allowed. Everything was done in a manner strictly in accordance with the requirements of the Discipline of the church. A great variety of fancy needle-work and handiwork of various kinds were prepared by the ladies and friends of the church. These were sold at the festival in connection with the usual material dispensed at a festival. The total receipts of the occasion were Six Hundred and Five Dollars and Fifty-five Cents, and the expenditures One Hundred and Twenty-four Dollars and Seventy-seven Cents, leaving a balance of Four Hundred and Eighty Dollars and Seventy-eight Cents as the net proceeds.

This nice sum was turned over to the building committee for the purchase of the seating which is still in use in the lecture room and in the class rooms of the church. This same Society, on Dedication Day, subscribed Seven Hundred Dollars toward the new church, and they paid it. During these twenty-five years, several Thousand Dollars have been gathered and judiciously applied by the Ladies' Aid of the church. They are doing their work with a will.

II. SUNDAY-SCHOOL.

"Feed my Lambs." John 21:15.

As might be expected, the Sabbath-School grew up with the church whose history we are endeavoring to sketch. About the same time that preaching services were established in the Lyceum, a Sunday-School was organized, 1845. Into this little room a few of the neighbors gathered the children of the village and the surrounding territory to instruct them as best they could, in the truths of the Holy Scriptures.

Mr. Joel Ebbert was the first Superintendent. He was helped in his work by about eight or ten teachers, some of whom did not belong to any church nor make any pretension to Christian fellowship. The school started and was conducted as a Union Sunday-School. It had at first about twenty-five or thirty pupils, but the number increased as the weeks came and went. The sessions were held in the mornings. Some of the first teachers were Messrs. Gideon Weikel, Amos Gearhart, James Rogers. John Finkbiner, James Gracey, Sr., and Daniel Latshaw, together with Mrs. Scypes, Miss Eliza Ann Rogers, Miss Sarah Lewis, Miss Ann Crater, and Miss Susan Dismant.

The undertaking flourished from the beginning and it kept up fully in numbers with the increase of population. The younger children read from their day-school books, also from The Union Primer and the Introduction to the English Reader. The Bible classes read from the Bible.

The school ran thus for about ten years. But in 1863, after the Union Meeting House became the property of the Methodists, the members of the Lutheran Church, who were identified with the school. withdrew, and soon afterward started a school under their own management on West Bridge Street in a school-house.

The Union school was held in the Lyceum for about six years; but it was transferred to the Union Meeting House after it had been fitted up for church purposes, in 1851. At first the sessions of the school were conducted during the summer months only, and closed during the inclement weather of the winter months. But after the streets and wide walks of the borough were better fitted up for travel, the school was kept open all the year, as now.

Great stress has always been laid on the work of the Sunday-School by the church. From the beginning of Methodism the Sunday-School has been regarded as the nursery of the church. Perhaps no other subject in connection with church work has been more frequently and emphatically reported at the Quarterly Conferences than the Sabbath-School. And perhaps none has been more effectively held up to the Throne of Divine Mercy in prayer than this one. It would be a little difficult to find a person in the church anywhere to-day who has not at some period of his or her life been a member of a Sunday-School, and been taught by a faithful teacher.

GROWTH.

Some figures, showing the growth of the school at different times as we have been able to cull them from the records, may not be out of place here. In 1850 the school numbered about forty or forty-five pupils, and, perhaps, eight or ten instructors. In the Quarterly Conference held at Coventryville, January 23, 1864, this table, showing the strength of the seven schools of the Circuit, is recorded:—

	No. Teachers	No. Scholars	Volumes in Library	Bible Classes	Infant Classes	Expenses of the School
Pottstown . . .	12	35	300	1	10	$35 00
Springville . . .	25	129	500	2	11	42 00
Nantmeal. . . .	21	121	150	3	12	30 20
Bethel	15	64	100	1	12	41 71
Coventry	15	70	250	1	20	45 00
Ebenezer	14	101	153	3	. .	22 00
St. John's . . .	9	55	125	2	8	15 00

In 1874, just ten years after this and the year in which
Spring City separated from the Springville and Bethel Circuit, and became a separate charge, the following occurs on
the Quarterly Conference minutes as reported by the pastor,
Rev. Eli Pickersgill:—

> Whole number of pupils enrolled.........176
> Average attendance 139
> Number of teachers..................... 24

At the First Quarterly Conference, held June 6, 1884,
the Superintendent, Mr. M. F. Sheeler, reported the number
of scholars in the school to be two hundred and ninety-eight,
and the average attendance for the Quarter, one hundred and
ninety-five; and that on May 30th of that year *every teacher
was present at the school, and taught his or her class.*

At the end of another decade, June, 1894, there were
three hundred and eighty-three scholars enrolled, with forty-
seven teachers and officers to carry on the work of instilling
religious truth into the minds of the young of the school.

ATTRACTIONS.

It may be in place here to note some of the wholesome attractions which the Sunday-School, along its history,
has held out to encourage the children to attend.   And first
we shall name Children's Day, the second Sunday in June.
This is a gala day for the little folks.   In short, it is their
day.   On this day they conduct a specially prepared programme, and they do it gladly, nobly, thus showing that they
are interested in the work.

Another attractive occasion for the Sunday-School children is the Christmas entertainment, which is usually held on
Christmas eve.   To this the children again eagerly contribute

their efforts. How glad they are to receive their gift box of candy, as well as to speak their pieces and to help in the singing!

The old-fashioned "Celebrations" have not yet quite lost their claim on Sunday-School folks. But now we call them "Picnics." The annual Sunday-School excursions are now added to the list of attractions for the young. And we may perhaps be pardoned here, if we say that one of the most noble acts of Christian fellowship that can be carried out, is to see a grand union Sunday-School excursion going out to have a pleasant time together. Let this continue. Let Lutherans, Reformeds, Methodists, all go together, and show to the non-church goers that the churches are working together harmoniously for the furtherance of the Master's kingdom.

Another powerful motive to enhance the claims of the Sunday-School is music. God very wisely placed into the souls of our children the ability to sing, to appreciate, and to love music, both vocal and instrumental. While the school was held in the Lyceum, the music was all oral. No melodeon or organ ever broke the silence of that sacred room. Teachers, scholars, all joined together and sang as best they could the soul-stirring melodies of those times, and the singing was helpful and encouraging.

FIRST INSTRUMENT.

So far as can be learned, the first musical instrument ever used in the Union Meeting House was a melodeon, some time about 1865. This instrument was used occasionally at the Sunday-School entertainments, and it was loaned for the occasion by Mr. John E. Lewis, and was played by Mr. Charles Weigel. The first instrument, an organ, was purchased about

1870, and used in the Sunday-School in the old church. When it came to the church, it was unpacked in the evening, and Miss Maggie Swindells who happened to be present, took a Sunday-School singing book and played this, as the first piece on the new instrument: "WE ARE MARCHING ON WITH SHIELD AND BANNER BRIGHT." The organ was placed in the northwest corner of the room, and was played by Miss Rebecca Vanderslice as the first organist. Other organs have been used since then, and in 1895 a fine upright piano, at a cost of Two Hundred and Seventy-five Dollars, was placed in the lecture room of the church for the use of the Sunday-School.

The following are some of the organists of the school: Mr. Griffith Knauer, Mrs. Rebecca (Vanderslice) Brown, Mr. Graves Shaner, Miss Kate Shaner, Mrs. Rachel (Peters) Oliver, and Mrs. Annie (Munshower) Saylor.

So far as can now be ascertained, this is the list of superintendents of the school, with the date when first chosen:—

IN THE LYCEUM.

Mr. Joel Ebbert, 1845 or 1846; Mr. G. A. Shryock, 1847; Mr. George Binder, 1849; Mr. David Wells, 1851.

IN THE UNION MEETING HOUSE.

Mr. David Wells, 1855; Mr. John Finkbiner, 1857; Mr. Edward Brownback, 1866; Mr. Samuel Gracey, 1867; Mr. F. R. Guss, 1872.

IN THE PRESENT CHURCH.

Mr. Samuel Gracey, 1873; Mr. M. F. Sheeler, 1884; Mr. F. M. Hunter, 1890; Mr. M. F. Sheeler, 1897.

The school now, 1899, enrolls three hundred and sixty-two, including forty-two teachers and fifteen officers. It has seven hundred and fifty volumes on its library shelves.

INFANT DEPARTMENT.

This school was organized in November, 1874, with fifty-four pupils, in class room No. 1. Miss Maggie Swindells was first Superintendent, and she was assisted at that time by Mrs. Rosa (Lutz) Ullman. In 1884 the school was removed to the basement of the church, where it remained until 1892, when it was transferred to its present quarters. The school now, 1899, numbers one hundred and twenty pupils. It is skillfully managed by Mrs. E. A. Bickel, Mrs. Mary L. Place, and Miss Ida Gracey.

MEETING FOR THE PROMOTION OF HOLINESS.

"Sanctify yourselves therefore, and be ye holy: for I am the Lord your God." Lev. 20:7. Also, "Follow peace with all men and holiness, without which no man shall see the Lord." Heb. 12:14.

The meeting for the promotion of this cardinal Bible doctrine was organized by Mrs. Mary E. Wood, wife of Rev. J. H. Wood, in July, 1873. She was assisted in the organization by Mrs. Alice Leech and Miss Maggie Swindells. Many members of the church have been helped and encouraged in these meetings. The meetings were held at first on Wednesday evenings, afterward on Sunday evenings before regular preaching services, as now. The meeting has been in charge of the following persons: Miss Maggie Swindells, Rev. James Swindells, Mr. John H. Setzler, Miss Lizzie Swindells, and at present Mr. Joseph Gracey conducts these helpful meetings.

III. CLASS MEETINGS.

We read in the Book of Malachi, 3:16, these words: "Then they that feared the Lord spake often one to another: and the Lord hearkened, and heard it." Ever since the year 1739, when Rev. John Wesley founded and lead the first class meeting which met weekly on Thursday evenings, the Methodists have regarded the class meeting service as a very valuable means of spiritual growth in their church. The church which has well-attended class meetings will have her aspirations onwards and upwards. The value of these meetings can scarcely be overestimated.

The first class leader in the church at Springville was Mr. David Wells, a farmer of East Vincent Township, who, in 1855, had a class of about a dozen members, the entire church. In 1857 the spiritual direction of this class was transferred to Mr. John Finkbiner, who still, 1899, advises, reproves, exhorts, and comforts the successes of this first class.

The second class was started in 1857 with Mr. Reuben Davis as leader. Here are the names of the other appointed leaders: Samuel Gracey, Caleb Hughes, Isaac M. Shantz, Simeon Keim, M. F. Sheeler, F. M. Hunter, Andrew M. Ortlip, J. G. Yeager, John McCann, Joseph M. Sheeler, Isaac M. Eberly, W. C. Urner, R. B. Hunter, and John F. Garber.

Mr. Eberly, for a short time, lead a class at Kimberton. When he left the district his class was dissolved.

IV. THE CHOIR.

"O come, let us sing unto the Lord; let us make a joyful noise to the rock of our salvation." Psa. 95:1.

Away back in the fifties there was no organized singing force in the church at Springville. Some person who could

CLASS LEADERS OF SPRING CITY M. E. CHURCH

do so, would start the singing, and the congregation would join in and sing as lustily as they could. The first effort ever made to organize a band of church voices here was made about the year 1861, by Messrs. John E. Lewis and David G. Wells. That choir was under the leadership of Mr. George K. Hoffman, a singing-school teacher of that day. They had no musical instrument to guide them except a C tuning-fork, which was skillfully used by the leader to pitch the tunes.

The choir met around among the houses of its members weekly, for practice, and they remained together until 1864, when the leader moved to Phœnixville. They sat together in the rear of the church between the doors. Among the choir singers' names of that time we find: Messrs. George K. Hoffman, John E. Lewis, David G. Wells, Samuel Gracey, Charles E. Weigel, Aaron Priest, Willis Bland, together with these ladies' names: Susan Hill, Henrietta Bland, Martha Gracey, Susan Gracey, Mary Sheeder, Martha Francis, and Jane Priest.

After 1864 the choir interest flagged until finally they did not meet for practice, and only congregational singing was used. Messrs. Samuel Gracey and Simeon Keim acted their part as Precentors in the singing until 1877. But after the year 1870, when the first organ was placed in the church, the instrument was used in the singing, and it was played first by Mr. Griffith Knauer, who sold the organ to the church. Other players for the choir at that time were Mrs. Rebecca (Vanderslice) Brown, Mr. Graves Shaner, and Mrs. Rachel (Peters) Oliver.

In the year 1877 the Rev. D. H. Shields, then pastor, organized the choir which, with its successors, is still rendering valuable and efficient service in religious worship. The organization as then effected, had for its leader Mr. William

Fox. and organist, Mrs. Rachel (Peters) Oliver. Among its members at that time are the names of Simeon Keim, J. R. Weikel, J. A. Guss, Jonathan Seazholtz, Mrs. Ida K. (Sheeler) Latshaw, Mrs. Florence (Sheeler) Peters. Mrs. Emma (Fox) Collins, and Mrs. Alice (Rogers) Latshaw. They sang first in the lecture room, and after 1879, where the choir is now located. The present Carpenter Organ was purchased in 1888 at a cost of Two Hundred and Eighty-eight Dollars and Seventy-five Cents, and the choir space was enlarged and fixed as it now is in 1893. Mr. William S. Essick succeeded Mr. Fox as leader, and served until Mr. Frederick A. Diemer, the present chorister, took charge in 1888.

The present choir consists of leader. Mr. Frederick A. Diemer; Organist, Prof. A. C. Anderson, together with these voices:—

Soprano—Mrs. Ida K. Latshaw, Mrs. Clara L. Mc-Michael. Mrs. Granville S. Tyson, Misses Annie L. Mowrey, Stella Livengood, and Cora E. Loomis.

Alto—Misses Grace B. Tyson, Martha Tyson, and Mrs. Loren Guss.

Tenor—Frederick A. Diemer, Dr. H. F. Jones, and Linford McMichael.

Bass—Willis O. McMichael, Brower H. Keiter, Granville S. Tyson, John H. Mowrey, Morris C. Keiter, and Loren Guss.

The choir meets weekly on Friday evenings at the church for practice. Such, briefly, is the history of the organized singing of the church. Up to the present choir no solos, duets, trios, quartets, nor choruses were rendered, nor was the organ heard during revival service. The soul-stirring melodies which are now so frequently and artistically ren-

CHOIR OF SPRING CITY M. E. CHURCH

dered were unknown to the older Methodists. They never enjoyed such vocal harmony.

The choir of to-day is under a very skillful and efficient management. The church owes these faithful Christian musicians a great debt of gratitude for their untiring services. There is great power in religious song properly rendered. When the facts are disclosed in heaven, many, no doubt, will be among the saved who can say that they were first impelled to lead a religious life through the inspiration of a hymn rightly sung.

V. EPWORTH LEAGUE.

The Spring City Chapter of the Epworth League, No. 3610, was organized September 8, 1890, with these officers:—

President—Reuben B. Hunter.

First Vice-president—Miss Sallie J. Diemer.

Second Vice-president—Mr. Joseph A. Coulson.

Third Vice-president—Mrs. Laura V. (Hildenbrand) Taylor.

Fourth Vice-president—Mrs. Anna (Smith) Cook.

Secretary—Miss Jane Noble.

Treasurer—Mr. Wayne Forrest.

As stated in the constitution, the object of the League is "to promote intelligent and loyal piety in the young members and friends of the church; to aid them in the attainment of purity of heart and in constant growth in grace, and to train them in work of mercy and help."

The membership are organized and are set to accomplish the ends attempted, under these departments of work: 1. Department of Christian Work. 2. Mercy and Help. 3. Literary Work. 4. Entertainment. 5. Correspondence. 6. Finance.

The members also bind themselves to hold one meeting a week for devotional services. They also hold a business meeting once a month. Entertainments of a wholesome and elevating character are also given at these business meetings.

The League has done a great deal of good thus far in its eight years' work. A wide field of usefulness is open to the membership of this valuable adjunct to the church. Their meetings are helpful and encouraging. This organization now numbers about one hundred members. Their motto is: "Look up! Lift up!"

THE JUNIOR EPWORTH LEAGUE.

This branch of League work was organized by Rev. D. Mast Gordon on May 12, 1894. Forty-nine members at once joined the work. They decided to hold their meetings on alternate Sunday mornings at 9.30 o'clock. This body of young Christian workers is under the direction of a superintendent who is appointed by the pastor of the church. They are instructed on the lines of Christian living, and in such other matters as will be a guide to the youth of the church.

VI. The Loyal Temperance Legion; or, Junior Temperance-School.

The Rev. N. D. McComas, in the year 1884, organized this body of little temperance workers, together with Mrs. Clara L. (Hildenbrand) McMichael as its first president. She held this position until 1886, when Miss Sallie J. Diemer took charge of the temperance instruction of the little folks, and she still is faithfully performing her delightful task. She and her loyal band are all happy in their efforts to do something for their Master.

The temperance catechism was at first used as a text-book of instruction; but, lately a wider range of Bible temperance instruction is given. This is mixed with a great deal of pleasant song singing.

The meetings were at first held in the infant room of the church on Saturday afternoons. Soon this room grew too small, and the class for the last ten years has met in the lecture room of the church on Sunday mornings.

Miss Diemer's temperance class is one of the attractive institutions of the church. It is well attended, and is very popular among the little folks. In the year 1889 this class won the banner for being the largest organized class of temperance workers in the country. Now, 1899, there are one hundred and fifty-three pupils' names on the roll, sixty-six of whom are pledged. During last year there were purchased and distributed six thousand five hundred and eighty pages of temperance literature by its members.

CHAPTER X.

BIOGRAPHIES.

"The steps of a good man are ordered by the Lord, and he delighteth in his way." Psa. 27:23.

JOHN FINKBINER.

This venerable gentleman, one of the oldest and most highly respected citizens of Spring City, both in and outside the church, was born in East Vincent Township, Chester County, Pa., August 8, 1818. He first saw the light of day on a farm now (1899) owned by Mr. Eber Finkbiner, a nephew of our sketch. He is the son of Jacob and Mary (Christman) Finkbiner. On the day that the boy John was nine months old, his father died.

Until he was seventeen years old the boy remained at home on the farm with his mother, who afterward married Mr. Frederick Yost.

The boy received his early education in the common schools of his district. Afterward he spent three terms at the Trappe Boarding School, kept at that time by Prof. Henry Prizer. While there the young man applied himself diligently in further pursuit of the Common English branches, and book-keeping.

As early manhood began to dawn upon Mr. Finkbiner, he had a great desire to learn the trade of carpenter, but in this vocation he was disappointed. As his physical frame at that time was not very robust, he began to stand in a store. First

JOHN FINKBINER, AGED 50 YEARS

he was employed (1837) by Mr. James Rogers, Sr., then for his brother Jesse Finkbiner, 1838-9, in Springville, at the locks just below where the drygoods store of A. F. Tyson now stands. After standing in a store in Philadelphia and at Sieglersville, Montgomery County, he went to farming.

He then engaged for his sisters, Misses Eliza Yost and Susan Finkbiner, on a farm in what is now Spring City, and he lived in the old farmhouse on Main Street, opposite the canal bridge. Here he remained until 1887, when the farm was cut up into building lots and sold. Now beautiful houses and streets occupy the once productive fields, especially along Yost Avenue.

Mr. Finkbiner joined the Lutheran Church at Zion's in his seventeenth year, where he remained in church fellowship until about 1855. During these years he was without a knowledge of saving faith in a Living Redeemer. But in 1840, while attending a Baptism at the Baptist Church in Phœnixville, he was convicted of sin, and he remained under this conviction at times until 1852, when he began in earnest to seek the pardon of his sins. While reading his Bible one day he received light, but he did not tell it to any one. Then he fell into spiritual darkness worse than before. He again sought the Lord in prayer, even going at 3 o'clock in the morning to Mr. George M. Binder on Hall Street, for prayer. While he was one day praying on the hay mow, he was directed by the Holy Spirit to retire to the house and read his Bible again. This he did, and his eyes fell on Isaiah 49, verses 13 to 17. As he read these verses his burden of sin rolled away, and he accepted the Lord as his personal Saviour amidst a flood-tide of spiritual happiness and ineffable joy!

In 1855 he joined the Methodist Episcopal Church in Springville, where he has since remained. He was one of the first trustees who bought the church in 1855, and he and Mr. David Wells, a drover, made themselves individually responsible for the debt of One Thousand One Hundred and Thirty-five Dollars which was against the church property. Mr. Wells failed to assume his share of the claim; hence Mr. Finkbiner himself paid the remaining debt, Eight Hundred Dollars, in the year 1868, thus freeing the church property from financial claims. In 1873, after the new church had been built, he again gathered up and paid all the outstanding claims against the church property, and took a lien on the same. Indeed, it is not too much to say that Mr. Finkbiner *has been the financial pillar of the Spring City M. E. Church.*

The spiritual services of this Christian gentleman to the church cannot be estimated. He has left behind him a monument of actual services which may well be followed by all. He has been a teacher in the Sunday-School since about 1847, except when he was superintendent, 1857 to 1866. He has been a Class Leader since 1857—now *over Forty Years.* He has been a member of the Trustee Board since 1855, and he has been their trusted Treasurer most of this time, as well as being Treasurer of the Sunday-School fund. His books show that he has been scrupulously careful of all the receipts and the expenditures which passed through his hands.

In conclusion it is proper to say that "Uncle John," as he is tenderly called, has been a very liberal contributor to all the needs of the church financially. He has lived a careful, clean, consciencious Christian life. The services of the church have always been a feast to his soul. He has wonderful power in prayer, and it will be a long time before the Spring City Methodist Episcopal Church will produce another "Uncle John" Finkbiner.

Rev. James Swindells.

Rev. James Swindells was born in England, January 25, 1805. His father had been an eminent Wesleyan local preacher, and hence he was trained up in the faith and belief of the same mode of worship. "Father Swindells," as he was familiarly called here, was early converted. and he gave himself earnestly to spiritual things.

He had been licensed as a local preacher in his native country. After he came to this country he still continued to preach. He was made a Deacon at Philadelphia in 1860, and at Norristown, in 1875, he was constituted an Elder. This title he maintained through life.

"Father Swindells" was a close Bible student through life. He held that, in order to have one's faith strong and unswerving, a Christian must feed his spiritual appetite on the Word of God. He, himself, read his Bible a great deal while on his knees. His preaching was sound, forcible, and full of the Word. He had a wonderful ability in quoting Scripture at all times. We have rarely met a person whose abiding faith was so implicit.

He was a strong advocate of Bible Holiness, and he took a great interest in the holiness meetings of the church while he was here. He died April 20, 1885. The Rev. Mr. Swindells was married in Manchester, England, to Miss Margaret Howe, in the month of May, 1828. Nine children blessed their home, which was always a pleasant one. The names of the offspring in order are: Martha. Maria, deceased; Rachel, deceased; Margaret. deceased: Elizabeth, Christian; James, deceased; William, deceased, and John T.

Two of the sons. William and John T., entered the ministry of the Methodist Episcopal Church. and forged their way to the front rank of their calling. The Rev. William was, for a number of years, Presiding Elder of the Northwest Philadelphia District of the Philadelphia Conference, and he filled the position with masterly ability. A great attachment always existed among the members of "Father Swindells" family for their sainted father.

REV. BENJAMIN LA PISH.

This prominent young man was born at Greensborough, N. C., April 15, 1868. He came to Pennsylvania with his parents soon afterward. He was converted at Friedensville M. E. Church, Lehigh County, in 1883, then joined the church at the above place. Afterward he joined the M. E. Church at Boyertown. He received his first exhorter's license from Rev. J. P. Duffey while here in 1886. At the Quarterly Conference held at Spring City, December 22, 1888, he received his first local preacher's license. On March 15, 1896, he was ordained Local Deacon by the Philadelphia Annual Conference. He then preached two years at the Yardley M. E. Church. During the summer of 1892 he supplied the pulpit at Landsdale. During 1896 and '97 he served the East Park Church at Thirty-third and Columbia Avenue, Philadelphia, and he is now (1899) at Bethel serving the Master and the people there.

In preparing himself for the life work which our brother so keenly felt was impressed upon him by the Holy Spirit, he attended the Pennington Seminary for four years. He then took a course of training at the University of Pennsylvania, graduating from the same in the class of '96 with the degree of A. B. Rev. La Pish is well equipped for a life of useful service in the cause of his Lord and Master.

LOCAL PREACHERS OF SPRING CITY M. E. CHURCH

On the eighteenth of June, 1896, our young man of God led Miss Clara Misson, of Philadelphia, to the hymeneal altar, where they were united as man and wife. George Benjamin, an interesting child, now makes their home joyous.

Rev. John Flint.

The subject of this sketch first saw the light of this world at Derby, England, in 1848, and came to the United States in 1862, and located at Philadelphia. He received the ordinary common school education of the schools of his district. He was converted in 1864, and joined the Front Street M. E. Church, Philadelphia, immediately. His faith and abilities soon led the brethren of his church to see that he was a proper person to receive license to exhort. Through timidity at that time he refused the call. But when he joined the Spring City Church, through the influence of the Spirit, he was led to see differently. He then accepted his exhorter's license from Rev. D. H. Shields, February 22, 1879, and on August 18th, of the same year, Presiding Elder Rev. George Cummings gave him his first license to preach.

Rev. Flint was ordained Deacon in 1885, and in 1889 he was ordained Elder. He has been staticned as minister as follows: Valley Forge, 1886 to 1893; Evansburg, 1890 to 1895, and since 1897 at Boyertown, Berks County. Prior to these regular appointments he preached every two weeks at Limerick, now Linfield, and served one year under Presiding Elder, Rev. William Swindells.

Besides his preaching services, Mr. Flint has always been a great worker in the Sabbath School. In this work he takes a special delight. He has been of much service in class leading also. Rev. Flint is still in the prime of life and he is doing excellent work for the Master. His sermons are full of helpful doctrine, truly Methodistic, and they are well received by his hearers. A well-equipped library of travel, history, biography, science, literature, art, and theology is skillfully used by the Rev. Mr. Flint in preparing himself for the pulpit.

On November 25, 1869, Mr. Flint and Miss Mary A. Newell wended their way to the parsonage of the Front Street Methodist Church, Philadelphia, where they were pronounced man and wife by the Reverend T. W. Simpers. Three children have played around their fireside: William J., deceased; Martha E., and M. Alice, who still survive.

REV. SAMUEL GRACEY.

The Rev. Samuel Gracey was born in the city of Philadelphia, August 25, 1835. His educational opportunities were narrowed down to a few terms in the Public Schools in East Vincent Township, Chester County, Pa. His father had a small library. Into this the boy Samuel plunged, and read and re-read everything upon which he could lay his hands. Mr. Gracey learned the trade of tailoring from his father, James Gracey. This trade has been the main support of his life.

During four years of Rev. Mr. Gracey's early life, he had access to Dr. Frederick Heckel's voluminous library of history, travel, and literature. The evenings of the young man were spent during this time in reading. He also took a lively interest in the debating societies then held hereabouts.

During the great revival of the winter of 1857 and '58, Mr. Gracey walked from Frick's Locks, on a rainy Saturday night, and he was soundly converted in the Methodist Episcopal Church at Springville, under the pastorate of Rev. Joseph Dare. This sterling event changed the whole life of our young man of twenty-two summers. He commenced then to study his Bible, and became a great reader. This habit of systematic reading he has kept up ever since.

In the year 1859 Mr. Gracey was recommended by his class as a subject for preacher's orders. Rev. James Cunningham, then Presiding Elder, gave the usual examination to Mr. Gracey, and licensed him, on January 25, 1859. On Sunday afternoon, January 26th, Mr. Gracey, in the presence of the Elder, preached his first sermon from Rev. 3:20. The Rev. Mr. Gracey has been a man of great and valuable service to the church of his choice. He preached the first Methodist sermon ever preached at Royersford. This was preached on a Sunday afternoon in Hobson's School-House, to an audience of Sunday-School workers. He organized the Hobson Union Sunday-School in 1857, and was its first Superintendent, which office he held for four consecutive years. He assisted in organizing the Garwood Sunday-School, and during two years he preached every four weeks in the Garwood School-House. He served for four years as Vice-president of the Joanna Heights Camp Meeting Association.

In 1884 Rev. Mr. Gracey was called to reorganize the Evansburg Methodist Episcopal Church, which then had lost its influence on the community. By appointment of the Presiding Elder, he served the church there until 1890. In 1887 a gracious revival broke out, and the church received a great spiritual quickening.

In 1890 he was sent to Valley Forge, where he administered the Word with his usual fidelity and pathos to the Methodist people of that historic spot. He remained here until 1895, when he was removed by the "time limit" of the Discipline. While here the Lord honored the services of his people by sending, during the winter of 1893, a revival which reached about *eighty souls*, many of whom are yet living a happy religious life.

Besides the above, the Rev. Mr. Gracey has helped at his home church during every revival that has been held since he joined the church in 1857. He has led a class at Spring City since about 1859. No pen can tell the amount of good which has been accomplished in the church by this devout man of God. He is the real type of a Local Preacher; always ready and willing to respond when he is asked to administer the Word. He has preached in most of the schoolhouses within a large radius of his home. He still wears the ministerial robes, and preaches whenever he has an opportunity to do so. His abilities as a Minister are assured from the fact of his numerous calls to the pulpits of other churches, as well as of his own. The pulpits of all the other Christian denominations with, perhaps, one exception in this vicinity, have also been filled by the subject of our sketch. Rev. Mr. Gracey celebrated the Fortieth anniversary of his ministerial services on January 25, 1899, in the presence of a good audience, by preaching from Deut. 8:2, "Thou shalt remember all the way which the Lord, thy God, led thee these forty years."

The sermon was full of beautiful and pleasant reminiscences of the work which has been done by this faithful, but humble, servant of the Redeemer, and it was eloquently delivered.

The Reverend Dr. Gracey and Miss Annie M. Grimm were united in the Holy Bonds of Matrimony at the Lutheran parsonage, Phœnixville, by the Rev. William Weaver, on December 10, 1856. Three children have come into their home: Ida I., William Hazel, deceased, and Susie C.

Rev. Andrew M. Ortlip.

This Reverend gentleman was born in Spring City, January 14, 1855, and was educated in the public schools of his native borough. He was converted during a revival at the M. E. Church on December 11, 1882. He joined the church in July, 1883. He received his first license to preach February 4, 1886. He served his church, doing what he could to advance the work of the Lord. In the year 1887 he felt impelled to carry the Gospel to the benighted people of Africa. He carried out his convictions, and on October 1st, of this year, he took passage on the steamer "City of Richmond," from New York, going by way of Liverpool, England. From Liverpool he sailed on the British steamer "Mandingo," and arrived at Cape Palmas, Africa, November 5th. He was soon sent about seventy-five miles interior to a place called "Tawky." Here he preached to the natives through the medium of a Liberian interpreter.

Often he would proceed to the shade of a large fruit tree, hang his umbrella on a branch of the tree, sing a hymn or two, and make a prayer. By this time a few of the astonished natives were around him when he opened the Scriptures to them.

While in Africa under Rev. William Taylor's Bishopric, Mr. Ortlip was ordained a Deacon, February 20, 1890, in the African Annual Conference, during one of its sessions at Cape Palmas, Liberia.

During his sojourn in Africa Rev. Mr. Ortlip sustained himself by first clearing the land of its trees and brush. He then planted the ground with pine-apples, plantains, sweet potatoes, rice, bananas, bread-fruit, cassava, coffee, cocoa-nuts, lemons, pawpaws, and other African products, for food.

While abroad he visited the Island of Maderia; also the Canary Islands. He left the self-sustaining missionary work of Africa after the lapse of three years. He returned home in September of the year 1890. At Cape Palmas he took sail on a German vessel, and came by way of Hamburg, arriving in New York on the above date. He and his family are at present (1899) living in the State of California.

On September 28, 1889, Mr. Ortlip proceeded to the clerk of the court of Maryland County, Republic of Liberia, and procured a marriage license in accordance with the customs of the place. The document is all made out in handwriting on one side of a half sheet of foolscap paper and bears the seal, "Republic of Liberia, Court of Quarter Sessions." We quote from the instrument as follows: "Whereas, Andrew Ortlip and Clara Binkley are desirous of being joined together in Holy Wedlock, and as there exists, to my knowledge, no legal barrier of the said Andrew Ortlip and Clara Binkley being joined in Holy Wedlock, it is, therefore, the privilege of any Ordained Minister of the Gospel, Judge, or Justice of the Peace of the aforesaid county and Republic to join the said *Andrew Ortlip* and *Clara Binkley* in the bonds of Holy Matrimony." The signature of J. Thomas E. Brooks is attached.

The Reverend B. E. Kephart, Presiding Elder of the District, pronounced the solemn rites of marriage between the above contracting parties at Cape Palmas, Liberia, on September 30, 1889. He gave a marriage certificate, written by hand, on a thin piece of tablet paper about five by eight inches in size, and the entire certificate is made out in seventy-four words.

Two boys have cheered the home of Reverend Mr. and Mrs. Ortlip. Their names are Titus and Paul.

The clerk of the court above, Mr. J. Thomas E. Brooks, is a jet-black colored man. So are all the government officials of the Republic of Liberia. They will not concede any rights whatever to a white man, not even selling him any ground.

REUBEN B. HUNTER.

This bright, promising young man was born in the borough of Spring City on July 13, 1869. He attended the Public Schools of his borough, and completed the course of instruction prescribed therein. His Diploma bears the date of 1885. Soon after graduating he connected himself with the Mowrey-Latshaw Hardware firm of which he is now a partner.

He sought and found the Lord in the year 1883, at Spring City M. E. Church. He immediately joined the church. During his church life of fifteen years he has been a Class Leader, a Teacher in the Sabbath School, and an active worker in the Epworth League.

He was licensed to exhort in the year 1891, and in 1898 he received his first commission as a Local Preacher and commenced to study the four years' course now prescribed for the Local Preachers. A life of useful opportunities lies before this enthusiastic young man of God.

On Christmas night, 1896, Rev. Mr. Hunter and Miss Anna M. Dunlap took upon themselves the marriage vow. Frank M., an interesting boy, now plays around the fireside.

CHAPTER XI.

PASTORS.

"How beautiful are the feet of them that preach the Gospel of peace, and bring glad tidings of good things." Romans 10:15.

An attempt is here made to produce the names of the pastors who have been more or less regularly appointed to preach at Springville-Spring City church. These dates have been carefully collected from the historical records of the church which are kept at the Book-room, No. 1018 Arch Street, Philadelphia. The Quarterly Conference records have also been consulted in making out the list. There most likely were other ministers who preached here, but in the main the list here produced is correct. The first name in the list is that of the Senior Preacher, or Preacher in Charge; the second is the name of the Junior, who acted under the direction of the Senior Minister:—

1845. Revs. Peter J. Cox, and John Shields.

1846. Revs. J. W. Arthur, and John A. Watson.

1847. Revs. J. W. Arthur, and John A. Watson.

1848. Revs. John C. Thomas, and John A. Watson.

1849, Revs. John C. Thomas, and James E. Meredith.

1850, Revs. George R. Crooks, and John A. Watson (supply).

1851, Revs. Allen John, and Jeshua H. Turner.

1852, Revs. James Hand, and Levi B. Bickley.

PASTORS WHO HAVE PREACHED IN THE PRESENT CHURCH

1853, Revs. James Hand, and William E. Manlove.

1854, Revs. Abraham Freed, and John F. Meredith.

1855, Revs. Abraham Freed, and Noble Frame.

1856, Revs. John Edwards, and William T. Magee.

1857, Revs. Joseph Dare, and N. W. Bennum.

1858, Revs. Daniel L. Patterson, and L. C. Pettitt.

1859, Revs. Daniel L. Patterson, and J. Brandreth.

1860, Revs. John B. Dennison, and Isaac Mast.

1861, Revs. John B. Dennison, and J. A. Watson.

1862, Revs. Valentine Gray, and Lorenzo D. McClintock.

1863, Revs. Joseph Aspril, and D. W. Gordon.

1864, Revs. Samuel G. Hare, and Samuel H. Reisner.

1865, Revs. Samuel G. Hare, and T. P. Thompkins.

1866, Revs. John Allen, and Adam L. Wilson.

1867, Revs. John Allen, and Thomas Harrison.

SPRINGVILLE AND BETHEL CIRCUIT.

1868-9, Rev. Jacob P. Miller.

1870-1, Rev. Richard Turner.

1872-4, Rev. John H. Wood.

SPRING CITY A SEPARATE CHARGE.

1874-7, Rev. Eli Pickersgill.

1877-9, Rev. David H. Shields.

1879-82, Rev. Joseph B. Graff.

1882-5, Rev. Nicholas D. McComas.

1885-8, Rev. Henry B. Cassavant.

1888-91, Rev. Josiah Bawden.

1891-4, Rev. Lucien B. Brown.

1894-7, Rev. D. Mast Gordon.

1897, Rev. Stephen H. Evans.

PRESIDING ELDERS.

The following Presiding Elders have looked after the general welfare of the church since the year 1855:—

1855-9, Rev. James Cunningham.
1859-63, Rev. T. J. Thompson.
1863-7, Rev. William L. Gray.
1867-72, Rev. J. Castle.
1872-3, Rev. W. H. Elliott.
1873-7, Rev. Peter J. Cox.
1877-81, Rev. George Cummings.
1881-3, Rev. William Swindells.
1883-7, Rev. Joseph Welch.
1887-91, Rev. J. F. Meredith.
1891-7, Rev. S. W. Thomas.
1897, Rev. William L. McDowell.

DISTRICTS.

The Springville-Spring City M. E. Church has been connected with the following Districts of the Philadelphia Conference:—

1845-57, Reading District, Pottstown Circuit.
1857-8, Reading District, Evansburg Mission.
1858-9, Reading District, Perkiomen Circuit.
1859-66, Reading District, Pottstown Circuit.
1866-8, Reading District, Coventryville Circuit.
1868-70, Reading District, Springville and Bethel Circuit.
1870-3, Central Philadelphia District, Springville and Bethel Circuit.
1873-4, Schuylkill District, Springville and Bethel Circuit.
1874-7, Schuylkill District, Spring City, a separate charge.
1877-81, Susquehanna District.
1881-99, Northwest Philadelphia District.

CHAPTER XII.

FINANCIAL POLICY.

The financial machinery of the church has not always been worked up to the systematic methods which are to-day employed. One of the marked instances of church success here is shown in the liberal hand which is everywhere seen in church work. But it was not always so. The people used to make their church contributions quarterly to their Class Leader. This was usually done at the class meetings. These contributed amounts were placed to the credit of the donor, on the class books. At the Quarterly Conferences the Class Leaders paid the amounts over to the pastors.

This method was in vogue at the Spring City church until the year 1879, when the envelope system of the present day was adopted. The plan in use now is that the collections for the Trustees' and the Stewards' Boards are all taken together. They then are divided. One-third of the money is given to the Trustees, and the balance is for the use of the Stewards. The most of the money which the Stewards receive goes for the support of the Gospel.

We append here the ingathering of the church for the fiscal year ending March 1, 1898.

STATEMENTS.

STEWARDS' FUND.

RECEIPTS.	DR.
To Balance from 1897.............	$21.03
To Envelope Collections...........	1554.38
To Lease Collections..............	308.89
To Extra Collections..............	30.00
	$1914.30

DISBURSEMENTS.	CR.
By Pastor's Salary................	$1200.00
By Trustees' Fund	621.06
By Elder and Bishops.............	56.00
By Moving Expenses..............	15.00
By Organ Boy....................	12.00
By Sacramental Wine.............	5.00
By District Steward	1.27
By Envelope Chart...............	1.00
By Balance in Treasury...........	2.97
	$1914.30

TRUSTEES' FUND.

RECEIPTS.	DR.
To Balance from 1897.............	$3.33
To Amounts from Stewards.........	621.06
To Subscriptions.................	91.24
To Amount from Ladies' Aid.......	24.95
	$740.58

DISBURSEMENTS.   CR.

By Interest paid $217.50
By Sexton's Salary 144.00
By Repairs 95.94
By Coal 88.73
By Book Racks 71.75
By Electric Light................. 69.03
By Insurance 23.75
By Taxes 21.54
By Water and Wood................. 8.34

$740.58

HOSPITAL FUND.

RECEIPTS.   DR.

To Church Contributions............$309.00
To Sunday-School Contributions 117.00
To Donations 60.00
To Ladies' Guild.................. 5.00

$491.00

DISBURSEMENTS.   CR.

By Money paid over to M. E. Hospital.$431.00
By Donations Forwarded............ 60.00

$491.00

MISSIONARY FUND.

RECEIPTS.   DR.

To Sunday-School $285.00
To Church 25.95
To Epworth League 25.00
To Junior Epworth League......... 17.00

$352.95

DISBURSEMENTS.   CR.

By Amount Paid to the Missionary
Board $352.95

                              $352.95

SUNDAY-SCHOOL FUND.

RECEIPTS.   DR.

To Amount Received First Quarter... $77.49
To Amount Received Second Quarter.. 83.37
To Amount Received Third Quarter.. 69.40
To Amount Received Fourth Quarter. 86.72

                              $316.98

DISBURSEMENTS.   CR.

By Books and Supplies.............$122.78
By Sundries 83.08
By Printing 12.00
By Balance in Treasury............ 99.12

                              $316.98

EPWORTH LEAGUE FUND.

RECEIPTS.   DR.

To Balance 4.25
To Missionary Boxes.................. 11.75
To Silver Collections 10.20
To Loose Collections................. 21.71

                              $47.91

DISBURSEMENTS.   CR.

By Amount to Missions..............$25.00
By Printing 9.50
By Donation to Organist............ 7.50
By Bouquets 2.00

By Donation (Shoes) 1.90
By Balance in Treasury............. 2.01

                                  $47.91

JUNIOR EPWORTH LEAGUE FUND.

RECEIPTS.	DR.
To Balance	$3.52
To Monthly Dues	7.05
To Other Collections	21.37

                                  $31.94

DISBURSEMENTS.	CR.
By Amount to Missions.............	$17.00
By Books	2.42
By Picnic Expenses	2.00
By Badges	1.75
By Supplies	1.20
By Missionary Boxes...............	75
By Balance	6.82

                                  $31.94

LADIES' AID SOCIETY FUND.

RECEIPTS.	DR.
To Balance	$65.45
To Dues During Year..............	86.55
To Market Receipts	27.22

                                  $179.22

EXPENDITURES.	CR.
By Amount paid Church............	$123.75
By Amount paid Parsonage..........	21.73
By Balance	33.74

                                  $179.22

THE POOR FUND.

RECEIPTS.	DR.
To Balance	$17.40
To Collections	34.00
	$51.40

DISBURSEMENTS.	CR.
By Expenses for the Poor	$25.60
By Balance in Treasury	25.80
	$51.40

THE LOYAL TEMPERANCE LEGION.

RECEIPTS.	DR.
To Balance	$44.69
To Loose Collections	20.18
	$64.87

DISBURSEMENTS.	CR.
By Sundry Expenses	$29.39
By Balance	35.48
	$64.87

THE CHOIR FUND.

RECEIPTS.	DR.
To Balance	$1.78
To Collections	5.36
	$7.14

DISBURSEMENTS.	CR.
By Special Music	$6.14
By Psalm Books	75
By Balance	25
	$7.14

1899.

REGISTRY OF THE METHODIST EPISCOPAL CHURCH OF SPRING CITY, PA.

Pastor.

REV. STEPHEN H. EVANS.

Local Preachers.

SAMUEL GRACEY.　　　　JOHN FLINT.
REUBEN B. HUNTER.

Exhorters.

MORRIS F. SHEELER.　　JESSE G. YEAGER.
JACOB K. JONES.　　　　JOHN F. GARBER.
JOSEPH A. COULSTON.

Trustees.

President, JESSE G. YEAGER.
Secretary, J. R. WEIKEL.
Treasurer, JOHN FINKBINER.

E. ALLEN BICKEL.　　　JOHN A. KEITER.
ENOS F. GRUBB.　　　　ANTHONY VANHOOK.
THOMAS G. WYNN.　　　URIAH B. GARBER.

Stewards.

MORRIS F. SHEELER.　　IRWIN I. WELLS.
JACOB K. JONES.　　　　WEBSTER C. URNER.
ALLEN A. BROWER.　　　JOHN H. DAVIS.
JOSEPH I. MOWREY.　　ANDREW F. TYSON.
A. LINCOLN TYSON.　　DR. J. WINFIELD GOOD.
FREDERICK A. DIEMER.　J. WALTER SHEELER.

Recording Secretary, WILLIS O. McMICHAEL.
Financial Secretary, JESSE G. YEAGER.
Recording Steward, W. C. URNER.
District Steward, M. F. SHEELER.

Class Leaders.

No. 1. JOHN FINKBINER..........*Sunday Morning.*
No. 2. MORRIS F. SHEELER.......*Sunday Morning.*
No. 3. SAMUEL GRACEY ....*Tuesday Evening.*
No. 4. WEBSTER C. URNER ......*Tuesday Evening.*
No. 5. JOHN F. GARBER ....*Thursday Evening.*
No. 6. JESSE G. YEAGER ....*Thursday Evening.*
No. 7. REUBEN B. HUNTER ......*Thursday Evening.*
No. 8. MISS SALLIE J. DIEMER,
       Temperance ....*Sunday Morning.*

Sunday-School.
Organized about 1845.

Superintendent, MORRIS F. SHEELER.
Assistant Superintendent, JOSEPH A. COULSTON.
Secretary, JOHN H. MOWREY.
Treasurer, JOHN FINKBINER.
Librarian, JACOB R. WEIKEL.
Chorister, LINFORD MCMICHAEL.
Pianist, MISS M. ALICE FLINT.

Infant Department.
Superintendent, MRS. E. A. BICKEL.
Assistants, MRS. MARY L. PLACE.
       MISS IDA GRACEY.
Organist, MISS IDA BICKHART.

Ladies' Aid Society.
Organized September 4, 1872.

President, MRS. MARY FLINT.
Secretary, MRS. MARY L. PLACE.
Treasurer, MRS. ANNIE M. GRACEY.

Epworth League.

Organized September 8, 1890.

President, WILLIS O. McMICHAEL.
Vice-president, CHARLES CRESSMAN.
Secretary, ALICE DUNLAP.
Treasurer, GEORGE NAYLOR.

Junior Epworth League.

Organized May 12, 1894.

President, DR. H. F. JONES.
Secretary, MISS LILLIE NOBLE.
Treasurer, J. OLIVER PLACE.

The Loyal Temperance Legion.

Organized 1884.

Leader, MISS SALLIE J. DIEMER.

Choir.

Organized 1877.

President, FREDERICK A. DIEMER.
Treasurer, BROWER H. KEITER.
Organist, PROF. A. C. ANDERSON.
Organ Boy, THOMAS G. MORGAN.

Ushers' Association.

Organized April, 1898.

President, A. LINCOLN TYSON.

Welcome Committee.

A. LINCOLN TYSON.   REUBEN B. HUNTER.
JOSEPH A. COULSTON.   FRANKLIN WADE.
CHARLES CRESSMAN.

Ushers.

ELIAS F. FORREST.   CHARLES DAVIS.
CLARENCE WALLEY.   ISAAC DUBSON.
ALBERT STOKES.

CHAPTER XIII.

OTHER CHURCHES.

"And other sheep I have which are not of this fold: them also I must bring, and they shall hear my voice; and there shall be one fold, and one shepherd." John 10:16.

We hereby give a short sketch of God's working among the other churches of the borough at Spring City. The older readers of this book well remember that at first the people of all opinions, faith, and creeds worshiped together. Many, no doubt, can well call to remembrance the happy times spent together in church and Sunday-School work in the Lyceum, and later, in the Union Meeting House. Hence we have gathered what few facts came within our reach, and we here give them for your perusal. In the scarcity of written records to be consulted, we have done the best we could to collect the facts which form these sketches.

ROYERSFORD METHODIST EPISCOPAL CHURCH.

On the first Sunday in May, 1857, at 2 o'clock in the afternoon, a Union Sunday-School was organized in the old Hobson's School-house, now torn down. Five officers, ten teachers, and forty-one pupils made up that school, which was held in the summer months, for several years. Mr. Samuel Gracey was its first Superintendent.

PREACHING.

The patrons of this school, as well as some of the neighbors, wished to have the Gospel preached. Their wants were

HOBSON'S SCHOOL-HOUSE

soon gratified. The announcement was made in the school that preaching services would be held after Sunday-School. The last Sabbath in May of 1861 was the time appointed for this religious worship, and Rev. Samuel Gracey, who then held his second annual local preacher's license, agreed to administer the Word.

Accordingly, at 3.30 P.M. on the above date, the Rev. Mr. Gracey stepped up to the teacher's desk, looked around, and he was pleased to see such a fine audience about him. The teachers and scholars had stayed after Sunday-School, and some of the nearby neighbors had come in also, to hear the first sermon ever preached at Royersford by a Methodist. The preacher's pulpit was not nicely upholstered; he did not preach from a large gilt-edged Bible whose marker hung down over the edge of the pulpit. There was no couch standing in the rear of the pulpit waiting to rest the weary minister after a laborious pulpit effort. No; nothing of the kind. Our preacher of the occasion simply started a hymn, and the audience joined in with him. After prayer had been offered, another hymn was sung. Then the speaker of the hour picked up a small Sunday-School Bible, went behind the old pine desk where many a day-school teacher had held dominion, and here, without a note or an eye-help of any kind, he poured the Gospel into the ears, and perhaps into the hearts as well, of his auditors.

Rev. Mr. Gracey continued these preaching services once a month until the Sunday-School closed in the fall. At nearly all the services the congregation filled the house. In very warm weather the services were held in the woods nearby. Twenty years were yet to elapse before any special effort was to be put forth to establish Methodism permanently in Royersford. The borough, which had been incorporated by

charter on June 14, 1879, still increased in population, and
at that time about Six Hundred people were within the borough limits. About forty or fifty people at the Ford were
members of the church at Spring City. These church-goers
were obliged to cross the river to attend all religious services.
This, in inclement weather, was not pleasant. Oftentimes
these devout followers of the sainted Rev. John Wesley were
deprived of religious services on account of the distance.

The project of having a Chapel built at the "Ford" was
frequently brought up in the official meetings of the church
boards. But nothing definite was accomplished until in April,
1881, when the pastor, Rev. Joseph B. Graff, called a meeting
of the male members in full connection with the church, as
he said, "for mutual consideration and advice." The subject
was well considered, and viewed from all sides. No decision,
however, was reached at that meeting. Consequently a second meeting of all the votaries of the church was convened,
by the pastor, on Friday evening, May 6th, following.

At this second meeting two projects were presented for
consideration. One was the erection of a Chapel at Royersford; and the other was the building of a Parsonage at Spring
City. The meeting was characterized by a free, harmonious
expression of opinion. Some argued for Chapel; others for
a Parsonage. When the vote was taken the result was:
Twenty-six had voted for a Chapel, and *Eight* for a Parsonage.
That settled it. The Chapel folks were delighted. They
could now look forward to the time when they, too, could
have religious services nearer home.

A CHAPEL BUILT.

Mr. Daniel Latshaw, a Christian gentleman connected
with the Mennonite Church, donated a lot of ground, 75 by

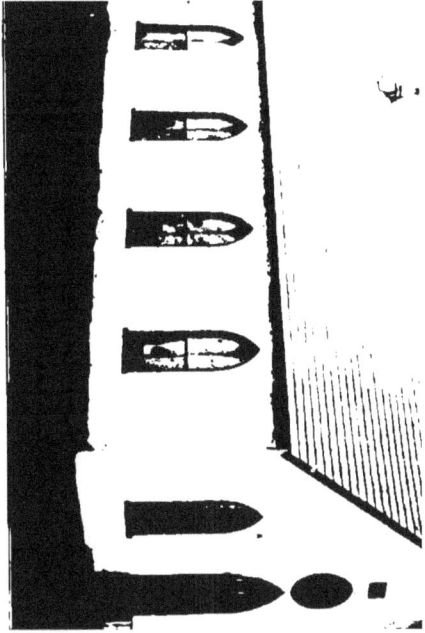

METHODIST EPISCOPAL CHAPEL, ROYERSFORD

200 feet, on which a neat, one-story brick Chapel was built. The present elegant church stands on the same lot. Messrs. M. F. Sheeler, Allen Rogers, John Bishing, William S. Essick, and S. B. Latshaw, composed the building committee to superintend the affair. On September 21, 1881, the cornerstone was laid with the usual services as prescribed by the Discipline. Presiding Elder, William Swindells, and Revs. G. D. Carrow, George S. Broadbent, William Bamford, John Bell, James Swindells, and Samuel Gracey, were present and assisted the pastor at the services. The work was pushed forward during the fall and spring. On Sabbath, March 5, 1882, the building, 32 feet 6 inches by 52 feet 6 inches, was solemnly dedicated to the worship of Almighty God in the usual way. On that day Bishop Matthew E. Simpson, D.D., LL.D., preached at Spring City at 10 A.M. Rev. J. G. Bickerton preached at the Chapel at 2.30 P.M., where the dedicatory services were performed. At 7.30 P.M., Presiding Elder William Swindells delivered the sermon at Spring City.

The entire outlay of the building and the furnishings was about $2800, and the whole church property at that time at Royersford, was valued at $3400. By Dedication Day the financial obligations were nearly all met.

PREACHING AT THE CHAPEL.

Preaching services were held now occasionally at the Chapel, especially on Sabbath evenings. Revival services were held regularly there, and preachers, exhorters, and lay members from Spring City went over and helped in the revivals. God graciously rewarded the services of these good people, by bringing men, women, and children into the fold in answer to faithful pleading in sermon, exhortation, prayer, and song.

ORGANIZATION.

When the Chapel mission was launched, it was under the control of the church at Spring City. There was but one board of church organization. The Royersford people were always well represented in the official boards, whose meetings were held at the "Mother Church," as well as the Quarterly Conferences. At these meetings a report of the working of the Chapel and the Sunday-School was always given.

SEPARATION.

When the Chapel was built and services held therein, it was not the intention of the Royersford people to leave the mother church. Their aim was to carry and present the Gospel to the community over the river. But the borough grew rapidly, and the church membership also increased. Times changed. New conditions presented themselves. These must be met. It was thought by 1886 that the cause of the Master could be served much better at the Ford if the church membership over there would retire from the home church and launch out on a wider field of action. Accordingly at the Fourth Quarterly Conference, held January 6, 1887, a vote was taken on the motion to ask the coming Annual Conference to send a pastor to Royersford during the ensuing year, and nineteen votes were cast in the affirmative. At the same meeting a motion was projected, asking *that Royersford be made a separate charge.* Eleven voted in favor of this motion; Eight opposed it.

MINISTERS.

At the Annual Conference that year, held at Philadelphia, Bishop R. S. Foster was asked to send a minister to the church at Royersford, and he appointed Rev. A. M. Viven as

ROYERSFORD M. E. CHURCH

their *first pastor*. About 80 members withdrew from the "Mother Church," and cast in their lot to serve the Lord "under their own vine and fig tree." The church now, 1899, enrolls three hundred and one full members, and eleven probationers. This is the list of pastors thus far:—

Rev. Abraham M. Viven, 1887, 1888, 1889; Rev. Joseph S. Lame, 1890, 1891, 1892; Rev. J. J. Timanus, 1893, 1894; Rev. Benjamin T. String, 1895, 1896; Rev. Andrew J. Amthor, 1897; Rev. Benjamin F. Powell, 1898.

A NEW CHURCH.

By the year 1891 the church membership had increased so much, and the attendance at the services had grown to such dimensions, that the Chapel was too small. The four years of its mission were now accomplished. It was torn down and the present handsome edifice stands on part of the ground on which the Chapel rested.

At the Quarterly Conference, held September 13, 1890, the following building committee was chosen and instructed to remove the Chapel and erect a new church in its stead: Messrs. Simeon Keim, S. B. Latshaw, William S. Essick, B. I. Latshaw, John Bishing, Rev. J. S. Lame, and Yelles C. Freed.

The new church was dedicated on March 20, 1892. Bishop Cyrus D. Foss was present on Dedication Day, preached a sermon, and performed the dedicatory services. The entire church property is now estimated at $35,000.

SUNDAY-SCHOOL.

"Wisdom is the principal thing: therefore get wisdom; and with all thy getting, get understanding." Prov. 4:7.

On Easter Sunday, April 9, 1882, the first Sunday-School was organized with Rev. N. D. McComas, as Superintendent;

William S. Essick, Assistant Superintendent; H. I. Ayres, Secretary; S. B. Latshaw, Librarian; J. J. Nix, Treasurer. At this first session of the Sunday-School there were present twenty-seven scholars, ten teachers, five officers, and one visitor; total, forty-two. Collection, Two Dollars and seventy-eight cents. Within one month from the date of organization the attendance had quadrupled. One hundred is the number reported at the Quarterly Conference, May 12, 1882.

The school has had the following Superintendents: Rev. N. D. McComas, 1882; Atmore Loomis, 1883 to 1887; William S. Essick, 1887 to 1894; Atmore Loomis, 1894 to 1896; Prof. George W. Bowman since 1896. The present strength of the school is three hundred and thirty-nine scholars and forty-nine teachers as per last Conference minutes.

INFANT DEPARTMENT.

It was at once found necessary here, as in other large schools, to institute a department of primary instruction. This was done, and now, 1898, one hundred and twenty-five pupils are in charge of competent teachers.

In 1896 a further division of an intermediate school was formed. This in part met the wants of the Junior Epworth League, which was then dropped.

CLASS HISTORY.

"Ye are my witnesses, saith the Lord." Isaiah 43:10.

In February, 1879, a number of church members over the river met in the parlor of Mr. John Bisbing, and held their *first class meeting*, with Mr. Simeon Keim as leader. At this meeting were S. B. Latshaw and wife, John Bisbing and wife, Albert Keffer and wife, B. I. Latshaw, Newton Latshaw, and others. This class held its meetings weekly around among its members until the church was finished in 1882, when its meetings were held in the church. Mr. Keim is still their trusted spiritual comforter and adviser.

A second class was formed in April, 1887, with Mr. John McCann as leader, and twenty-six members. On January 16, 1888, a third class of twenty-six was formed, with their pastor, Rev. A. M. Viven, as leader. The fourth class dates from March 1, 1889. Rev. A. M. Viven took charge of this class of fifty-nine probationers and one full member. Class No. 3 had been given to Mr. William S. Essick. James Spear took care of the fifth class which began to hold its meetings from 1893. It started with twenty-seven members. The present, 1898, class register will be found under the Registry of the Church.

EXHORTERS.

"Rebuke, exhort with all long suffering and doctrine." 2 Tim. 4:2.

Messrs. William S. Essick, afterward a local preacher, Simeon Keim, Harry I. Ayres, and John F. Garber were exhorters when the church organized in 1887.

OFFICIAL BOARDS.

We find from the church records that on April 8, 1887, a special meeting of the male members of the church was called by the pastor, Rev. A. M. Viven. At that meeting the following official boards were appointed to serve until the first Quarterly Conference could approve them:—

Trustees—Messrs. Simeon Keim, Atmore Loomis, Samuel B. Latshaw, B. I. Latshaw, Samuel C. Freed, John McCann, John Bisbing, Yelles C. Freed, and H. Bessinger.

Stewards—H. I. Ayres, William S. Essick, Albert Keffer, Josiah J. Nix, William Cook, John Hause, and William Bruner.

The Recording Stewards of the church have been Mr. H. I. Ayres, 1887 to 1893; Mr. Peter C. Fritz since 1893.

REVIVALS.

In reference to the enlargement of the church membership, the "Daughter Church" had somewhat the same experience as the church from which she sprang. In the second year of their existence a gracious revival broke out. At this revival Satan's work was badly hindered at Royersford. About Sixty or Seventy souls found their way to the altar, and God, for Christ's sake, spoke pardon to their souls.

Rev. Mr. Viven was ably supported by the exhorters and the entire membership in the work of soul saving. God wonderfully answered prayer, and some of the strong, reliant membership of to-day came to a knowledge of soul salvation in the revival of the winter of 1888-9. We notice that fifty-nine members were in the probationers' class at this time.

A second marked influx of souls came to the church during the pastorate of Rev. J. S. Lame. This revival was not so much the spasmodic outbreak of religious fervor, as a continuous ingathering time. During the three years of this gentleman's stay among the good people over the river, the membership of the church was nearly doubled. People sought and found the Lord at all seasons of the year, summer as well as winter. By one's and two's they came and were gathered to the church which the Lord purchased with his own precious blood.

Choir.

This faithful band of musical voices which have been so helpful in the religious exercises, started and grew up with the church. The credit of the organization of this church function, belongs to the late Mr. Harry I. Ayres, whose valuable services were always freely tendered to the church of his choice. He gathered about him a collection of voices, trained them, and in April, 1887, they began to lead the congregation in singing. Mr. Ayres was the first leader of the choir.

Some of the names of the first choir singers are: Misses Ella Latshaw, Eva Essick, Sallie Richards, Ida S. Morey, Mrs. Maggie Newborn, Messrs. John Hause, Simeon Keim, Joseph S. Newborn, and A. W. Berks.

LEADERS, ETC.

The choristers who have wielded the baton since Mr. Ayres laid it aside, are: Messrs. Charles E. Minker, Willam S. Essick, Harry W. Murray, Luther Bush, George Shule, Harry W. Murray, and Charles E. Minker, who is the present musical director. Under Mr. Minker's guidance there are now twenty voices, classified as follows:—

Soprano: Mrs. Charles Conover, Mrs. Mary Matthews, Mrs. Kate Minker, Misses Stella Usner, Millie Shule, Ella M. R. Latshaw, Ida Raiser, Ora Murray, and Nilla Newborn.

Alto: Misses Alice Berks, Jessie Latshaw, Eva Bowman, Mary Freed, and Grace Usner.

Tenor: Messrs. A. W. Berks, Luther M. Bush, and George Shule.

Bass: Charles E. Minker, Harry M. Murray, and Lloyd Strouse.

ORGANS.

While the congregation worshiped in the chapel, a cabinet organ was used for all church and Sunday-School purposes. But when the church edifice of to-day was built, the present handsome Bohler pipe organ was also erected. Mr. Samuel Bohler, of Reading, Pa., made and put this complex musical instrument in place at a cost of Twenty-five Hundred Dollars. The instrument is run by a water motor, and has done faithful services.

Those who have occupied the organ stool during singing, and whose trained fingers have passed over the finger-boards of the organs, are the following: Mrs. Alice Latshaw, who played in the chapel. Then Mr. Elmer Latshaw, Misses Eva Essick, Ida Richards, Anna Brown, and at present, Miss Ida Richards again.

FINANCIAL POLICY.

As the members of the official boards of the Daughter Church had already been in the same relation at the Mother Church, they at once knew how to effect a strong organization when the separation came. The experience gained at Spring City was at once of service to them. It was only natural to adopt a financial policy which had already proved to be in harmony with the desires of the church. So the church at the Ford have adopted, and are using, the envelope plan, which urges the members to contribute weekly or monthly through the envelope, such amounts as can be given by every member who is in a position to support the Gospel. The collections are gathered into one common fund. At the distribution Five Dollars are deducted from the gross amount, then forty-five per cent. of the balance is given over to the Trustees, and the remaining fifty-five per. cent. passes into the hands of the Stewards' Board for the purpose of meeting their obligations. We append below the financial ingathering of the church for the conference year ending March 1, 1898.

FINANCIAL STATEMENTS.

STEWARDS' FUND.

RECEIPTS.	DR.
To Envelope Collections	$1608.76
To Loose Collections	315.97
To Special Collections	431.16
To Ladies' Aid Society	100.00
To Epworth League	53.50
To Sunday-School	25.00
To Other Sources	121.26
	$2655.65

DISBURSEMENTS.	CR.
By Pastor's Salary	$1100.04
By Collector's Commission	60.00
By Bishop and Elder	44.00
By Trustee Board	1146.40
By Parsonage Rent	180.00
By Note Paid	77.30
By Freight and Incidentals	47.91
	$2655.65

TRUSTEES' FUND.

RECEIPTS.	DR.
To Stewards' Board	$1146.40
To Organ Lessons	4.50
	$1150.90

	DISBURSEMENTS.	CR.
By Interest Paid		$507.94
By Sexton		240.00
By Gas and Water		64.70
By Organist and Tuning Organ		78.00
By Coal		87.45
By Repairs		112.73
By Insurance and Sundries		60.08
		$1150.90

Sunday-School Fund.

	RECEIPTS.	DR.
To Balance on Hand		$7.90
To Regular Collections		208.68
To Missionary Collections		159.83
To Other Collections		84.98
		$461.39

	DISBURSEMENTS.	CR.
By Expenses of School		$290.74
By Missionary Fund		159.83
By Balance on Hand		10.82
		$461.39

Ladies' Aid Society.

	RECEIPTS.	DR.
To Balance		$3.46
To Dues		120.17
To Sociable Receipts		46.02
To Other Receipts		33.83
		$203.48

DISBURSEMENTS. CR.

By Amounts Paid Out..............$202.28
By Balance on Hand................ 1.20

$203.48

EPWORTH LEAGUE FUND.

RECEIPTS. DR.

To Balance $6.41
To Dues 56.27
To Other Receipts................. 67.04

$129.72

DISBURSEMENTS. CR.

By Stewards' Board................ 53.50
By Singing Books.................. 27.00
By Donations to the Poor........... 9.80
By Sundries 32.89
By Balance 6.53

$129.72

JUNIOR EPWORTH LEAGUE.

RECEIPTS. DR.

To Balance $9.77
To Picnic Proceeds................. 17.51

$27.28

DISBURSEMENTS. CR.

By Amounts Paid Out..............$27.28

$27.28

POOR FUND.

DR.

To Collections $38.48

CR.

By Disbursements $38.48

CHOIR FUND.

DR.

To Personal Contributions..........$128.91

CR.

By Disbursements $128.91

BENEVOLENCES.

RECEIPTS.	DR.
To Missionary Church	$50.17
To Hospital	23.00
To Other Collections	106.00
	$179.17

DISBURSEMENTS.	CR.
By Missionary Board	$50.17
By Hospital	23.00
By Other Benevolences	106.00
	$179.17

1887. 1899.

REGISTRY OF ROYERSFORD METHODIST EPISCOPAL CHURCH.

Pastor.

REV. BENJAMIN F. POWELL.

Local Preachers.

JOHN K. MANSUR.   HENRY BROOK.
ROBERT AMSTER.   JOSEPH DIEHL.

Exhorters.

SIMEON KEIM.   JAMES B. RICHARDS.
PROF. GEORGE W. BOWMAN.

Trustees.

President, SIMEON KEIM.
Secretary, B. I. LATSHAW.
Treasurer, S. B. LATSHAW.

JEREMIAH CULLER.   H. B. GEISINGER.
ARTHUR RICHARDS.   JOHN K. MANSUR.
JOHN BISBING.   ATMORE LOOMIS.

Stewards.

GEORGE W. BOWMAN.   PETER C. FRITZ.
WILLIAM COOK.   WILLIAM BRUNER.
JAMES SPEAR.   WILLIAM RAISER.
THOMAS SPENCER.   HARRY MUNSHOWER.
HARRY RICHARDS.   WARREN MANSUR.
LORENZA MORGAN.

Recording Steward, PETER C. FRITZ.
District Steward, PROF. GEORGE W. BOWMAN.

Sunday-School.

Superintendent, GEORGE W. BOWMAN.
Assistant Superintendent, JAMES B. RICHARDS.
Secretary, ARTHUR E. RICHARDS.
Treasurer, MRS. MARY MATTHEWS.
Librarian, S. B. LATSHAW.
Choister, CHARLES E. MINKER.
Organist, MRS. ALICE BERKS.

Intermediate Department.

Superintendent, MRS. B. I. LATSHAW.
Assistants, MRS. J. H. BIXLER.
    MISS KATE LOOMIS.
Chorister, H. W. MURRAY.
Organist, MRS. ALICE BERKS.

Infant Department.

Superintendent, MRS. ALICE LATSHAW.
Assistants, MRS. WILLIAM COOK.
    MRS. WILLIAM LATSHAW.
Chorister, MISS MILLIE SHULE.
Organist, MISS LILLIE RICHARDS.

Ladies' Aid Society.

Organized April 7, 1887.

President, MRS. ALICE LATSHAW.
Secretary, MISS KATE LOOMIS.
Treasurer, MRS. JOHN NEWBORN.

Epworth League.

Organized June 8, 1892.

President, JAMES RICHARDS.
Secretary, MISS FLORENCE LOOMIS.
Treasurer, J. H. BIXLER.

Choir.

Organized April, 1887.

Chorister, CHARLES E. MINKER.
Organist, MISS IDA RICHARDS.

Ushers.

ATMORE LOOMIS.   S. B. LATSHAW.
H. B. GEISINGER.

CHAPTER XIV.

THE EVANGELICAL LUTHERAN CHURCH.

EARLY PREPARATION.

"Thy word have I hid in mine heart, that I might not sin against thee." Psalm 119:2.

The first preaching in Springville by Rev. Martin Luther's followers was in Mechanics' Hall. So far as can now be ascertained, back in the sixties the Rev. Henry S. Miller, who was then stationed at the Trappe, came here and preached at intervals. Rev. William Weaver of Phœnixville, also preached in the Hall. We are also informed that the Rev. Mr. Smith of the Trappe, came here occasionally, and broke the Word of Life to those who were eager to hear, and be profited by spiritual advice. A Rev. Mr. Gearhardt of Phœnixville, came and administered the Word also, according to the ceremonies of the Lutheran Church. The Revs. Laitzel of Pottstown, and Kohler of the Trappe, also preached in the Hall.

ORGANIZATION.

Thus, as the borough grew in size, the Lutheran services also became more frequent. In September, 1872, the Rev. Jacob Neff, who had been previously called, came and took charge of the congregation at Zion's Lutheran Church. He resided in Spring City, and it was only natural for this devoted minister of God to take a special interest in the welfare of that part of his flock among whom he lived, and had daily converse. And while he was alive to the best interests of the

SPRING CITY LUTHERAN CHURCH

good people at Zion's, and did all in his power to cater to their best church necessities, he saw that the time was now ripe to make an effort to establish a church in the borough. The way was open, and it was in his province to organize the Spring City Evangelical Lutheran Church. This he did.

BUILDING PURCHASED.

In the fall of the year 1872 the school-house which, now a dwelling, stands in the rear of the present parsonage, was purchased from the School Board, and fitted up for church purposes. The title to the property bears the date of January, 1873. The building was soon appropriately dedicated according to the rites and ceremonies of the church. The Rev. Henry S. Miller, of Phœnixville, was present, preached the dedicatory sermon, and performed the dedicatory services.

CHARTER.

The Lutherans now had a regular preaching place of their own, and here they held all their church and Sunday-School services under the guidance of their new pastor, Rev. Mr. Neff. The church prospered, the congregation increased, and these faithful, energetic followers of the Lord were happy. So they proceeded until the year 1875. They now began to realize the fact that, if they were incorporated, it would be much better for the church. Accordingly in the above year the church authorities applied to the court of the county for a charter of incorporation. This was granted, and it bears the date of August 12, 1875. Things now went on. Five years more of diligent services were before them in the school-house.

For five years yet the Rev. Mr. Neff has to preach the saving Word of Life to those who inclined to spiritual things.

Then the end came. The congregation grew too large to be
accommodated in their narrow quarters. A more commodious
and modern church edifice was needed. And it was with
these children of the Lord, just as it always is. The Lord
opened up a way in answer to faithful prayer. A new church
must be built. All efforts are pushed in that direction. Plans
are devised and they must be executed.

A New Church.

"Heaven is my throne, and earth is my footstool: what
house will ye build me? saith the Lord." Acts 7:49.

The spring of the year 1879 found the Lutheran people
in the midst of building a new house to be solemnly given
to the services of the Lord of Hosts. The corner-stone was
laid with appropriate ceremonies, on a very warm day, July
24, 1879. On through the summer, fall, and winter following, the merry sound of skillful mechanics was heard, all doing
well their part to produce the beautiful structure which now,
1899, still stands at the corner of Church and Chestnut
Streets.

Dedication.

By the month of June, 1880, the building was ready for
dedication. The services which commenced on Saturday
evening, June 26th, were completed on Sunday, June 27th.
On Dedication Day the Rev. C. W. Schaeffer of the Theo-
logical Seminary, Philadelphia, preached the Dedicatory sermon, and performed the rites of the dedicatory services to a
crowded house. The following clergymen were also present
and participated in the services: Rev. O. K. Kepner of Pottstown, Rev. O. P. Smith, of Trappe, Montgomery County; Rev.
Kahler, Rev. Strodach, and the pastor, Rev. Jacob Neff.

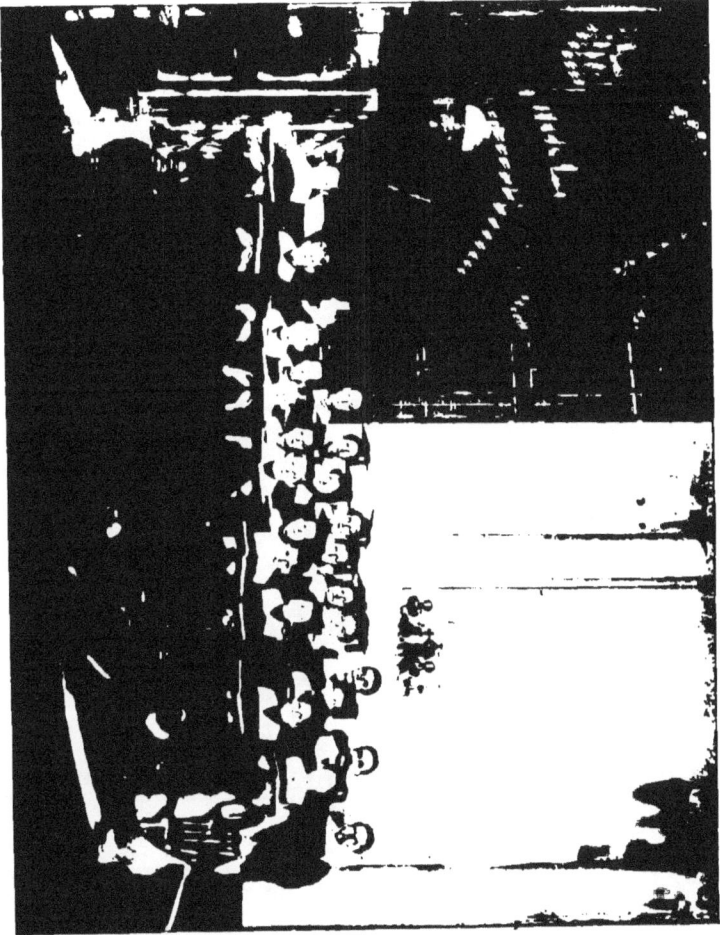

CHOIR OF THE LUTHERAN CHURCH

The building is of stone, 46 by 77 feet in size, two stories high, and is of that style of architecture known as Ionic. The lower story is 12 feet high; the upper, 21 feet. The upper room seats Five Hundred people. It is supplied with solid white-walnut curved seats, which are cushioned. The room is beautifully frescoed. In short, the building is an up to date church edifice in every way, and it is a credit to the town, and a special credit to the church and congregation that worships within its shrines. The structure cost about Nine Thousand Dollars.

CHOIR.

"I will sing unto the Lord as long as I live: I will sing praise to my God while I have my being." Psa. 104:33.

Davis Hause, Esq., who took a lively interest in the affairs of his church, was one of the promoters of the choir. This band of Christian voices was organized in the year 1872, in the church. Mr. Hause was the choice of the choir as their first chorister. The names of some of those first singers who stood by their leader are: Mrs. Minerva (Diemer) Atkinson, Mrs. Alice (Diemer) Wood, Mrs. Sallie (Diemer) Christman, Mrs. Mary (Diemer) Leidy, Mrs. Martha (Fleming) Kline, Mrs. Annie (Lichty) Wells, Mrs. Mary C. (Schmoll) Rosenberger, Mrs. Christian W. Wagoner, Messrs. William J. Wagoner, John H. Custer, Frederick Diemer, L. H. Rosenberger, Esq., and David G. Wells.

The organists are Mrs. Minerva Atkinson, Mrs. Mary (Simon) Winner, Mrs. H. Margaret (Taylor) Latshaw, Mr. D. H. Bickhart, Misses Lydia Diemer and Jennie Custer.

When Mr. Hause was done beating time for these vocal musicians, he handed his prerogative to these choristers: Messrs. Frederick Diemer, L. H. Rosenberger, Esq., William W. Emery, Henry Latshaw, and Frederick Strahle.

The successors of the above organization made the religious services of their church resplendent with their vocal harmonies, up to the time of the organization of the present musical organization.

VESTED CHOIR.

This band of vocal musicians, the first of its kind in our town, owes its origin and existence to the efforts of the Rev. Aden B. MacIntosh, the pastor of the church. He gathered about him this body of young voices, organized and trained them for singing in the public congregation. They made their first appearance, in full vesture, at the six o'clock meeting on Christmas morning, 1896. Since this date the services of the church have been enlivened by the young folks, who take a great delight in their part of the religious work. The twenty-eight voices now in the choir are classed as follows: Nineteen sing soprano; five, alto; and four, bass.

INSTRUMENTS.

Up to the year 1893 a cabinet organ was used in the choir; but, in the above year, the handsome and deep-toned pipe organ now in use, was built. This instrument cost Eighteen Hundred Dollars. It is propelled by a water motor.

TENEMENT HOUSES.

In the year 1888 four cozy tenement houses of brick were erected on the north side of the church lot, along Hall Street. The old church edifice had already been fitted up for a dwelling, thus making five dwelling houses, which are now added to the church property. The estimated value of all the church property is about Twenty Thousand Dollars.

GROWTH.

When the Spring City church separated from Zion's in 1892, there were about two hundred members in this vicinity who enrolled their names on the books at the borough church. Now, 1899, the membership has grown to about two hundred and fifty who are communicants. Their number is steadily increasing, and while some of the membership are either removing to other quarters or are taken to their heavenly home, others are filling up the ranks.

PARSONAGE.

As stated in another place, house No. 130 on New Street, was the first furnished Methodist parsonage. Strange to say, this same house was the Lutheran parsonage between the years 1874 and 1886. In this year the fine brick parsonage which still stands on Church Street, was built by the Ladies' Aid Society of the church, at a cost of Three Thousand Dollars. Rev. Mr. Neff and family then occupied the new parsonage until his death.

When Rev. Mr. Neff came here in 1872 to preach his trial sermon, he was not married. But on November 20, 1872, he married Miss Sarah B. Yount, and on the 22d of the same month he brought his bride to Spring City. They took up their abode with Dr. F. W. Heckel on the Schuylkill Road, where they remained until April, 1873. They then went to housekeeping on South Main Street, east side, in the single frame house on the Yeager-Hunter Stove Works lot. They remained at this place one year, when they moved in April, 1874, to No. 130 New Street, one end of Mr. Philip Simon's house. They lived at this place until the new parsonage was completed. Then they went thither and occupied the new building.

SUNDAY-SCHOOL.

"My son, if thou wilt receive my words, and hide my commandments with thee, so that thou incline thine ear unto wisdom, and apply thine heart to understanding, then shalt thou understand righteousness, and judgment, and equity; yea, every good path." Prov. 2:1, 2, 9.

As already stated in another place, the first attempt to train the children hereabouts in the truths of the Bible, was made in the Union Sunday-School. Here all religious denominations worked side by side in the Lyceum, and afterward in the Union Meeting House. But things are changed. To George M. Binder belongs the credit of promoting the idea of the first Lutheran Sunday-School in Springville. One day in the spring of the year 1863, he met Mr. Daniel R. Shalkop, and said that he thought it would be nice to have a Lutheran Sunday-School. "I have no fault to find with the Methodists," he said, "but as we are Lutherans, it will be a good idea to have a Sunday-School of our own. We can have our school in the afternoon, as the Methodists have theirs in the morning; so we will not conflict with one another." Such was the conversation.

Mr. Binder's idea was carried into effect. A meeting was soon called in the school-house, which then stood on West Bridge Street. Here then was organized the First Lutheran Sunday-School, with these officers:—

Superintendent, George M. Binder; *Secretary*, Davis Hause, Esq.; *Treasurer*, Andrew Ortlip; *Chorister*, Davis Hause, Esq.; *Librarian*, Samuel B. Shalkop.

About thirty or forty pupils were present at the start, but the number grew steadily larger. Some of the teachers who had charge of the youth of that day were Gideon Weikel,

George M. Binder, Andrew Ortlip, Daniel R. Shalkop, William J. Wagoner, Elmore Shaner, Samuel B. Shalkop, Mrs. Mary (Shalkop) Wagoner, Mrs. Mary Ann (Finkbiner) Taylor, Mrs. Margaret (Finkbiner) Shenkle, and Miss Tille Hallman.

Here, in the Western school-house, the school was held in the summer months, and in the winter the school was closed. It increased and prospered under the skillful management of these early pioneer teachers. Money was collected and a library was purchased so that the children might read wholesome literature. For three years the school remained in the school-house. In the spring of 1866 it was removed to the basement of Mechanics' Hall, where it remained until 1873. It was then transferred to the church's new quarters in the rear of the present parsonage, and afterward to the present church building.

SUPERINTENDENTS.

Mr. Binder was the choice of the school as superintendent for two years, when he was followed by Mr. Jacob Sheeder. This is the list with the date of their first election, when the date could be ascertained: Mr. Gideon Weikel, Frederick Diemer, 1875; Rev. Jacob Neff, 1876; Mr. Frederick Diemer, 1877; Mr. Gideon Weikel, 1879; Mr. William J. Wagoner, 1880; Mr. H. K. Giles, 1881; Mr. Frederick Diemer, 1883; Mr. Jonas Bickhart, 1884; Rev. J. Neff, 1886; Mr. George D. Peters, 1897.

ORGANISTS.

Some of those whose trained fingers made the organ pour forth its sweet music during the singing of the school, are: Mrs. H. Margaret-Taylor-Latshaw, Mrs. Martha Keim, Miss Lydia Diemer, Mrs. Kate E.-Bean-Hepler, Mrs. Lillie-Finkbiner-Slichter, Mrs. Lallie-Wagoner-Rosen, Mrs. Lillie-Wagoner-MacIntosh, Mrs. Florence Peters, Mrs. Kate-Peters-Floyd, Mrs. Arete C.-Wagoner-Emery, Mrs. Minnie-Elliot-Davis, Misses Jennie Custer, Lizzie Rogers, and Mr. D. H. Bickhart.

TREASURER.

The present Treasurer, Mr. C. W. Wagoner, has enjoyed the confidence of his contemporary laborers in the school to a great degree. He has been their Treasurer since 1874, twenty-four years.

THE SCHOOL OF 1899.

The teachers whose efforts to train their children in the first school of 1863, have nearly all done their work in this world. Many of their pupils are still living; but the Sabbath-School instructors themselves have gone home to the other world. Their places are now occupied by others. The beautiful and attractive Sunday-School rooms of to-day are still filled with a goodly number of bright, merry boys and girls. Earnest, devoted teachers meet their scholars Sabbath after Sabbath; and in an atmosphere which is all vocal with the sounds of the musical voices of children reciting lessons, the Sabbath-School workers are doing their best to instruct, to train, to help.

The roll of to-day numbers about Two Hundred and Fifty teachers and scholars, properly divided into classes and skillfully taught. An infant department of about sixty-five is also in training. Well-earned success has crowned faithful effort in the Sabbath School.

REV. ADEN B. MACINTOSH

Rev. Jacob Neff.

I hope the reader will not grow out of patience here, if we pause a moment, uncover our heads, and pay our tribute of respect to the excellent worth of this Reverend Gentleman. During the twenty-three years of his faithful ministry here, he endeavored to serve his people well. Always alive to the best interests of the church of his choice, he served those whose spiritual interest he had so much at heart, with a devotion which was unswerving. In his skillful hands, guided by the Holy Spirit, the work of his heart and life grew. The church grew. Many, no doubt, will be the souls who, in glory, will call him blessed.

Kind, sympathetic, and tender-hearted was he always. He continuously tried to have a helpful word for the discouraged. He was the first minister that served the church here. He died, loved and respected by all of his acquaintances, on January 13, 1896, leaving behind him a record of unswerving fidelity to his Master.

New Pastor.

For about four months after the death of Rev. Mr. Neff, the church was served by supplies as they could be obtained from time to time. After a few months of service the church extended a ministerial call to the present pastor, Rev. Aden B. MacIntosh, who accepted and took charge of the church and congregation on June 1, 1896. Rev. Mr. MacIntosh is still the faithful leader of his flock. His sermons are full of power and persuasive eloquence. The work under his persistent efforts is growing.

1872.　　　　　　　　　　　　　1899.

OFFICIAL REGISTER OF THE SPRING CITY EVANGELICAL LUTHERAN CHURCH.

Pastor.

REV. ADEN B. MACINTOSH.

Church Council.

President, MR. CHARLES PETERS.

Secretary, MR. J. EDGAR DIEMER.

Trustees.

W. HARVEY BROWER.　　　JOHN H. CUSTER.

MILTON LATSHAW.

Elders.

WILLIAM H. ROBINSON.　　GEORGE O. KEITER.

GEORGE D. PETERS.

Deacons.

WILLIAM C. WILLIAMS.　　J. EDGAR DIEMER.

JACOB F. LEIDY.

Sunday-School.

Organized 1863.

Superintendent, GEORGE D. PETERS.

Assistant Superintendent, CHARLES S. WAGONER, ESQ.

Secretary, W. HARVEY BROWER.

Treasurer, C. W. WAGONER.

Librarian, ANDREW EISENBISE.

Organist, MRS. FLORENCE PETERS.

Infant Department.

Superintendent, MRS. KATE FLOYD.
Assistants, MRS. L. H. ROSENBERGER.
MRS. WILLIAM ROBINSON.

The Luther League.

Organized January 23, 1894.

President, J. EDGAR DIEMER.
Secretary, MISS JENNIE CUSTER.
Treasurer, W. HARVEY BROWER.

Junior Luther League.

Organized October 3, 1894.

President, MRS. KATE FLOYD.

The Ladies' Aid Society.

Organized March 25, 1879.

President, MRS. KATE FLOYD.
Secretary, MISS M. NORMA WAGONER.
Treasurer, MRS. CHARLES PETERS.

The Vested Choir.

Organized December 25, 1896.

Chorister, REV. A. B. MACINTOSH.
Organist, MISS JENNIE CUSTER.
Treasurer, PAUL NEFF.

CHAPTER XV.

THE FIRST REFORMED CHURCH OF SPRING CITY.

EARLY PREACHING.

"So shall my word be that goeth out of my mouth: it shall not return unto me void, but it shall accomplish that which I please, and it shall prosper in the thing whereto I sent it." Isaiah 55:11.

Mr. James Rogers, Sr., was a personal friend and great admirer of the Rev. Alfred E. Shenkle who was stationed at East Vincent Reformed Church from 1848 to 1869. At one of the frequent interviews held by these gentlemen, Mr. Rogers gave the Rev. Mr. Shenkle a warm invitation to come and preach at Springville. This the Reverend gentleman agreed to do. In the fulfillment of his promise, we find that on November 29, 1848, he entered the Lyceum, stepped behind the quaint pulpit, gave out his text, and preached an earnest sermon to a fair-sized audience. *This was the first sermon delivered here by a Reformed Minister.*

On December 5th of this same year, the Rev. Mr. Shenkle preached again. He preached frequently at intervals during the winter at the Lyceum, and he kept up the practice for several years. In March, 1849, he held a series of revival services there in which several persons became interested in their spiritual welfare, professed conversion, and joined the church at East Vincent. As Rev. Mr. Shenkle's private records, taken at that time show, quite an awakening on the subject of religion was experienced among his auditors. Some people are yet in the church laboring for the Master, who were gathered from the darkness of sin at this time, and started on their pilgrim journey.

Through the efforts of "Father Shenkle" the first seeds of religious truth were sown hereabouts, in accordance with the ceremonies of the church in which this devout minister of the Gospel has spent the greatest part of his life.

Between the years of 1851 and 1855, Mr. Shenkle also occasionally held up the banner of the Lord in the Union Meeting House. As occasion presented itself, he embraced the opportunity of delivering to the people the message which his Master inspired him to present. In this modest way was started the nucleus of the thriving Reformed Church which was in the providence of the Lord, to become one of the great Religious Institutions of Spring City.

The Rev. Maxwell S. Rowland, who succeeded "Father Shenkle" at East Vincent, 1860 to 1881, also came here and administered the Word of God occasionally in Mechanics' Hall. It was only natural as the borough continued to grow and prosper, that the number of communicants of the Reformed Church should also increase proportionately. This was the case; but they still retained their church relationship at "The Hill Church" as it was called.

As time elapsed, preaching services became more frequent at the Hall, so that the people here might have the opportunity to worship according to the rites and ceremonies as laid down by the Sainted Revs. Ulrich Zwingli and George Michael Weiss, of the early church in the United States. Thus church matters moved forward until the year 1881, when a forward step was taken by the Reformed people.

In 1881 the Rev. D. W. Ebbert was called to the pastorate of the East Vincent Reformed Church. He took up his residence in Spring City. While here he soon became impressed with the fact that the time had now arrived for the organization of a charge in the place of his residence.

About this time Rev. Mr. Ebbert began to preach regularly on Sunday evenings in the Hall. This venture at once revived the spiritual interest of his flock in church work. His preaching was attractive, forceful, eloquent. The people flocked around him, and to do with a will "what their hands found to do." The Lord worked with them. The congregation grew; the number of communicants increased also.

ORGANIZATION.

In March, 1882, just one year after Mr. Ebbert's advent, a second forward step was taken. A committee, consisting of Messrs. Joseph Keeley, Thomas Francis, Francis Latschar, Henry Francis, and Henry J. Diehl, was appointed to confer with the East Vincent congregation on the subject of separation from the "Mother Church." The result of their mission was the granting of Thirty Letters of dismissal to the members of this church, with the understanding that they would found a congregation in Spring City. Further steps were taken, and by April, 1882, these Thirty Members of the "Mother Church" and seventeen others, making forty-seven in all, were banded together and admitted to full standing. Thus they launched forth in the good work as *The First Reformed Church of Spring City.*

The first Elders were Messrs. Casper S. Francis, Davis Kimes, and George Snyder. The first Deacons were Messrs. Henry Francis, James Rogers, and Andrew McMichael.

They still held all their services in the Hall. These were now more regular, mostly in the afternoon and evening, with the Sunday-School session in the afternoon also. Thus they

FIRST REFORMED CHURCH, SPRING CITY

worked and grew until they moved into the new church. On Christmas Day, 1884, the congregation moved from the Hall into the lecture room of their handsome new church on Chestnut Street, and then held their first service in their new church home.

NEW CHURCH.

The corner-stone of the new church edifice was laid on June 21, 1884, and the church was dedicated on April 2, 1885. The venerable Dr. J. H. A. Bomberger, President of Ursinus College, preached the dedicatory sermon to a crowded house. Other ministers present were D. E. Klapp, D.D.; Revs. H. F. Spangler, S. P. Mauger, E. D. Wettach, G. S. Sorber, B. F. Davis, L. K. Evans, and the pastor, Rev. D. W. Ebbert.

Much of the credit of this munificent church enterprise is due to Messrs. Joseph Keeley, Henry Francis, and Mrs. Mary E. Kelley, who contributed liberally of their means to the support of the same. The edifice, a stone structure, is 41 by 74 feet in size, two stories high, seats 300 people on elegant opera chairs, and it cost about *Fourteen Thousand Dollars.* The lower room is for Sunday-School and other purposes, as is the case in all the churches of the town. The entire church property is valued at Thirty Thousand Dollars.

PRESENT STRENGTH.

Three Hundred and Two communicants now, 1899, surround the Lord's Table to partake of the emblems of his broken body and shed blood. The financial ingatherings for church purposes during the fiscal year ending May 1, 1898, were Two Thousand Three Hundred and Twenty-one Dollars and Sixty-six Cents; and for the same period, the benevolences of all kinds make the fine sum total of One Thousand Four

Hundred and Ninety-two Dollars and Fifty-two Cents. This shows that these disciples of the Lord give of their substance to his cause with an open hand.

THE SUNDAY-SCHOOL ASSOCIATION.

This is one of the auxiliaries of the church, and has for its mission about the same range and scope of work as is performed in the other churches by their Ladies' Aid societies. It sprang into existence during Mr. Ebbert's ministry in 1882. It was started as a financial organization in connection with the Sunday-School; hence its name. During its Sixteen Years of existence it has collected and applied to various church purposes over *Four Thousand Dollars*. The organization now numbers upwards of One Hundred Members, who tax themselves ten cents a month as dues.

PASTORS.

The Rev. D. W. Ebbert guided the spiritual aspirations of these good people until July, 1887, when he resigned. He was followed on January 1, 1888, by Rev. L. K. Kremer. This gentleman remained in charge until August, 1890, when he was gathered to reap his heavenly reward. The pulpit again was filled by supplies from various places, until a call was extended to the Rev. Calvin U. O. Derr. He took up the work in June, 1891. Under his efficient and indomitable labors the church greatly prospered. He was an eloquent and fluent speaker, and he had a great hold on his congregation, as well as on the people generally.

A large ingathering of souls was the outcome of his efforts among these arduous people. Rev. Derr energetically ministered to his congregation until he too was called home to his reward in heaven. He died after a brief illness on March 12, 1897, mourned not only by his church and congregation, but by the people of the town as well. This brilliant young man will not soon be forgotten by the members of the First Reformed Church of Spring City. After the lapse of a few months, the present genial pastor, Rev. J. M. S. Isenberg, was called to the pulpit. He was ordained in October, 1897. The spiritual skies of the Reformed Church are bright.

SEPARATION.

The church here did not feel that they were strong enough to launch out for themselves until the year 1891. Up to this time they had been connected with the East Vincent Church, but now they effect a peaceful separation, and since then they have been a separate charge.

FAIRVIEW PARSONAGE.

About the year 1890, the present pretty cottage which bears the above name, was erected by the church for the home of the pastor. Previously the dwelling which joins the present parsonage grounds on the east, had been built and used as the pastor's dwelling. The present home of their pastor is a roomy, well adapted building for its purpose. It is equipped with hot and cold water, bath-tub, etc. It cost Three Thousand Three Hundred Dollars, and it is an up-to-date dwelling. A stable is also on the parsonage lot. The view from the parsonage is picturesque and beautiful.

The Choir.

"Sing unto the Lord with thanksgiving; sing praise upon the harp unto our God." Psa. 147:7.

A few years after banding the membership of the church hereabouts into church fellowship, it was thought necessary to have also an organized singing force. The value to a church of trained musical voices was appreciated by the good people of the Reformed Church, and an effort was accordingly placed on foot to bring together the younger members who were inclined to that part of the work, with a view of having them lead the singing in the public services. This worthy purpose was carried into effect. We find that at a stated meeting of the Consistory of the church, held on May 6, 1890, Mr. W. Ashley Mowrey moved "to have a choir organized, and that Mr. George Diemer be seen regarding leadership, and the organization of the same." This was during Rev. Mr. Kremer's last year of the pastorate.

Mr. Diemer accepted the honorable charge placed in his hands by his church, and set himself about at once to gather around him those who were qualified for singing, and upon whom he could rely for help in conducting that part of the public worship which, in all ages, has been so soul-inspiring, namely: singing. His effort was a success. His abilities were indorsed by the Fourteen Members who constituted the *First Choir* of the Reformed Church.

Mrs. Alice-Lichty-Spangler was the choir's first organist. When the choir, after rehearsal, made their debut before the audience, they had Twelve Voices, besides two cornetists. Miss Lichty occupied the organ stool until she wedded the Rev. Mr. Spangler a few years afterward. Miss Nettie Anderson now is the organist. This band of singers meets for rehearsal at the present time on Thursday evenings; but prior to Mr. Eiler's leadership, Friday evening was choir night.

Mr. Diemer continued to be the chorister of his church until July of 1898, when he resigned on account of a weak throat. Mr. J. F. Eiler has swung the baton since that time. Mr. Eiler has around him Fifteen voices: six soprano, four alto, two tenor, and three bass. These now stimulate the public worship with their harmonious strains.

Sunday-School.

"My son, keep my words, and lay up my commandments with thee." Prov. 7:1.

A Sunday-School was organized in the Hall in June, 1881, with about thirty pupils, and it has been successfully conducted ever since. At the present time a very flourishing school is conducted in which the children are instructed in the truths of the Bible. About Four Hundred and Forty scholars are enrolled in this school. They are divided into classes in the usual way. This school is in a very flourishing condition.

SUPERINTENDENTS.

Here is the list of those to whom this responsible calling has been intrusted. The date succeeding each name is the time when first chosen: Rev. D. W. Ebbert, June, 1881; Mr. George Snyder, February 1, 1887; Mr. John M. Latshaw, January 8, 1889; Rev. L. K. Kremer, January 10, 1888; Mr. George Snyder, February 5, 1889; Mr. F. R. Bossert, January 6, 1891; Mr. William H. Blanchford, January 3, 1893; Rev. C. U. O. Derr, January 2, 1894; Mr. William M. Stauffer, January 7, 1896; Mr. Oliver T. Taney, January 3, 1897; Mr. James MacIntire, May 8, 1898.

1882.   1899.

REGISTRY OF THE FIRST REFORMED CHURCH OF SPRING CITY.

Pastor.

REV. J. M. S. ISENBERG, B.D.

Consistory.

Elders.

JAMES MacINTIRE.   ISAAC S. OBERHOLTZER.
FRANCIS LATSCHAR.   W. CARROLL TAYLOR.
F. W. GOSHOW.   WILLIAM F. STEPHEN.

Deacons.

S. E. FRICK.   H. E. LATSCHAR.
HARRY SAESER.   JONES DIEMER.
H. A. HECK.   O. J. SCHUBERT.

Sunday-School.

Organized June, 1881.

Superintendents, JAMES MacINTIRE.
Assistant Superintendents, SAMUEL JONES.
                           MRS. G. M. DIEMER.
Secretary, O. T. LEE.
Treasurer, H. EMMETT LATSCHAR.
Librarian, HARRY DRUCKENMILLER.
Organist, MRS. F. EDNA (DIEMER) HECKEL.

Infant Department.

Superintendent, MRS. S. EDGAR FRICK.
Assistants, MRS. FRED. L. STAUFFER.
           MRS. WILLIAM A. FRANCIS.
Organist, MISS EMMA V. ALBRIGHT.

Christian Endeavor Society.

Organized October 13, 1890.

President, HARVEY A. HECK.
Secretary, MISS MARY S. EACHES.
Treasurer, MISS LILLIE KIMES.

Intermediate Christian Endeavor Society.

Organized February 12, 1894.

Superintendent, REV. J. M. S. ISENBERG.
Secretary, MISS FREDRICKA MCVEIGH.
Treasurer, MISS CLARA K. EACHES.

Missionary Society.

Organized 1888.

President, MRS. GEORGE M. DIEMER.
Secretary, MISS ANNIE J. DIEHL.
Treasurer, JAMES MACINTIRE.

Sunday-School Association.

Organized 1882.

President, MRS. MARY E. KEELEY.
Secretary, MRS. S. E. FRICK.
Treasurer, MRS. F. WILLIAM GOSHOW.

Spring City Men and Boys' Club.

Organized 1894.

President, REV. SAMUEL GRACEY.
Secretary, M. RUSELL STOKES.
Treasurer, F. WILLIAM GOSHOW.

The Choir.

Organized May 6, 1890.

Leader, MR. J. F. EILER.
Organist, MISS NETTIE B. ANDERSON.

CONCLUSION.

Before drawing this little effort to a close, we shall adventure to deduce a fact or two in reference to the labors of the pioneer Methodists of the Spring City Church. We beg leave here to ask the question: "What are the elements of success which have crowned the efforts of God's people here, not only in the Methodist, but in the other churches, as well?" In answering this question, we have learned from the records that one of these is—

EARNEST PRAYER.

The people of God here have always been enthusiastic in their supplication to a Throne of Mercy. Men and women in the past have spent much time on their knees, as they still are doing. In revival efforts persistent prayers were always full of faith. Without faith it is impossible to please God. Their faith in many instances was so strong that they would not let go until God sent the blessing. They wrestled like Jacob of old until they saw the increase. Men and women prayed mightily; Satan's foundations shook; God won the victory.

DEVOTION TO THE CHURCH.

The reports of the pastors to the Quarterly Conferences frequently mention the devotion of the church membership to the different services. When the church doors opened for a prayer service, the people were there. At class meeting times these same Christian people responded to roll-call, and gave their testimony in honor of their Lord to the best of their ability. Preaching services were also a spiritual feast to them. At the Quarterly Meeting Love feast and preaching services, there always was a spiritual uplifting.

The different charges were always anxious to have the Quarterly Meetings at their church, for this meant a good time for everybody who was spiritually inclined.   What though a few members from the other charges were present on Saturdays at Quarterly Conference, and stayed for the Sunday services! This mattered not, for the encouraging testimonies at Love Feast always helped somebody.   The Love Feasts of those days were held with closed doors.   These services were too sacred to be interrupted after they had commenced.

The Lord works through human instrumentalities.   He does not send a host of angels down from Heaven to gather sinners into the fold; but he reaches men and women by means of Christian men and women.   The old Methodists knew this; hence they tried to lead lives of consecration to the Master. When revival time came the church was up and ready for the work.   Everybody was aglow!

HOLD ON THE COMMUNITY.

A little retrospective glance over the field of labor in which the Methodists have pushed their claims in this section of the Schuylkill valley for the last fifty years, reveals some facts of interest to us.   The early settlers in Montgomery, and also in northern Chester County, were mostly of German origin.   These sturdy, frugal tillers of the soil brought with them their spitual advisers, as well as their long-established notions of religious piety, from the Fatherland. As they had been either Lutherans or members of the Reformed Church at home, so they were here.   They built churches on both sides of the river in the counties mentioned. Children were reared in the piety and belief of parents.   As the early pioneers dropped the weapons of this world, their

offspring took up the work of the church where they found
it, and kept pushing it along with the pace of progress. The
descendants of the early churches still exist over the hills and
among the valleys in this vicinity.

So it will be seen that when the first efforts were put
forth to sow the seeds of Methodism among the people here,
they were confronted with the fact that very many of the
sons of men had been already associated in church fellowship.
Their names already formed a part of some church roll of
membership. Mr. John Wesley's followers then found that
they undertook no little task when they attempted to plant
another society of church fraternity on soil which had already
been so well cultivated. But at the work they went. They
had faith in their cause, and, perhaps, more faith in their
Heavenly Father. So they labored on, never tiring, and apparently never growing weary in well-doing. Men, women,
and children as well, were rescued from sin, one by one. The
ransomed were vigorously urged to take upon themselves the
vows of church relationship. That God blessed their labors
is certain. The fruits of Gospel labors on all sides are apparent to-day.

As the disciples of Mr. Wesley look over the parish on
which many a well-fought battle with sin was won, they have
great cause for congratulation. How often have they seen,
around the altar of prayer in the church, the contests of sin
settled once and forever, on the side of God and righteousness. Victory always perched on the right banner, when a
poor trembling sinner gave his case into the hands of a
merciful Saviour.

The results of to-day show that the Methodist Episcopal
Church at Spring City and at Royersford have a combined
membership of about Six Hundred and Seventy-five souls on

their church records. To this may easily be added an additional church-going numbership of *Four Hundred* more whose sympathies are, in some way, drawn toward the faith and belief of this church. Place these two numbers together, and it is at once noticed that a combined church-going population in the two towns of upwards of One Thousand different people in the course of the year, entered her sanctuary, take their seats, and hear the Soul-saving word proclaimed from her sacred desk.

The two towns have a population of about *Twenty-five Hundred* each, making a total of *Five Thousand* who live within their combined precincts. With these facts before us, we are now able to see to what extent the influence of Methodism to-day reaches the masses of the people. One Thousand out of Five Thousand attend the Methodist Church. That is, one-fifth, or an average of one out of every five, is helped to right thinking along religious lines at these churches. Is this not remarkable! If the reader will stop to ponder, he or she will learn that this is a record of the triumph of the gospel of Methodism which exists in very few, if any, places in this section of the State. In how many towns, or rural sections, with which you are acquainted, can you see such a result? This is not said in the way of boasting; but simply as an historic fact which is shown by the records.

We have mentioned these facts, not to whip the churches of to-day with even a feather, for certainly much earnest, laudable effort is launched forth in the name of the Lord, for the purpose of saving the lost. The present aggressive attitude as shown in all the churches combined, goes very far to account for the observance of the Sabbath, the moral tone of the community, and the general well-being of the people as well. Surely the future outlook of God's work here has the rainbow of promise encircled over it. It now remains for all those who assume the obligation of church fealty to measure up to the full stature of their allegiance to Almighty God, in order to perpetuate the purity of the sanctuary. May their power over the unconverted still increase! The Lord surely wants his people to be a holy people.

Now, kind reader, we have told our story. We have presented to your gaze the facts as best we could. The book is not all that we could wish it to be. There may be, and no doubt there are, many interesting facts and coincidences which would have added greatly to the value of the volume; but they have not come within our reach. Try to read the book with a generous eye. Do not criticize too severely. An effort has been made to state the facts plainly, yet humbly. We know that it is much easier to act the part of an iconoclast than to produce something of greater merit. The work is now commended to your kind consideration.

INDEX.

www.ingramcontent.com/pod-product-compliance
Lightning Source LLC
Chambersburg PA
CBHW030315270326
41926CB00010B/1380